MW00824511

JUST PLAY

Other Redleaf Press books by Miriam Beloglovsky
Loose Parts for Children with Diverse Abilities

With Lisa Daly
Loose Parts: Inspiring Play in Young Children
Loose Parts 2: Inspiring Play with Infants and Toddlers
Loose Parts 3: Inspiring Culturally Sustainable Environments
Loose Parts 4: Inspiring 21st Century Learning
Early Learning Theories Made Visible

With Michelle Grant-Groves
*Design in Mind: A Framework for Sparking Ideas,
   Collaborations, and Innovation in Early Childhood*

Miriam Beloglovsky

Inspiring Adult Play
In Early Childhood
Education

 Redleaf Press®
www.redleafpress.org
800-423-8309

Published by Redleaf Press
10 Yorkton Court
St. Paul, MN 55117
www.redleafpress.org

© 2023 by Miriam Beloglovsky

All rights reserved. Unless otherwise noted on a specific page, no portion of this publication may be reproduced or transmitted in any form or by any means, electronic or mechanical, including photocopying, recording, or capturing on any information storage and retrieval system, without permission in writing from the publisher, except by a reviewer, who may quote brief passages in a critical article or review to be printed in a magazine or newspaper, or electronically transmitted on radio, television, or the internet.

First edition 2023
Cover design by Louise OFarrell
Cover photographs by Wayhome Studio,/Stock.adobe.com, Cookie Studio, K8most
Interior design by Louise OFarrell
Typeset in Adobe Minion Pro
Interior photos by Stockbusters (p. 61), EdNurg (p.73), David Prahl (p. 98), Lightfield Studios (p. 112), Tyler Olson (p. 117); all other photos by the author.
Printed in the United States of America

29 28 27 26 25 24 23   1 2 3 4 5 6 7 8

Library of Congress Cataloging-in-Publication Data
Names: Beloglovsky, Miriam, author.
Title: Just play : inspiring adult play in early childhood education / by Miriam Beloglovsky.
Description: First edition. | St. Paul, MN : Redleaf Press, 2023. | Includes bibliographical references and index. | Summary: "Play is crucial in adulthood because it fosters adaptiveness, creativity, role rehearsal, and mind-body integration. Just like children, when adults engage in play and creative endeavors, they can find that childlike center that cultivates happiness and joy. They will be equipped to work with children, design effective curricula, understand children and increase empathy, create playful leadership opportunities, and make significant changes to their programs and organizations"— Provided by publisher.
Identifiers: LCCN 2023004103 (print) | LCCN 2023004104 (ebook) | ISBN 9781605547770 (paperback) | ISBN 9781605547787 (ebook)
Subjects: LCSH: Play. | Early childhood education—Activity programs. | Early childhood teachers—Training of. | Early childhood teachers—In-service training.
Classification: LCC LB1139.35.P55 B459 2023 (print) | LCC LB1139.35.P55 (ebook) | DDC 372.21—dc23/eng/20230224
LC record available at https://lccn.loc.gov/2023004103
LC ebook record available at https://lccn.loc.gov/2023004104

Printed on acid-free paper

I dedicate this book to the people who play for joy—
who find playfulness in their lives and recognize its
capacity to increase creativity and learning.

Contents

Introduction

Sometimes there comes a moment in life that changes everything you do and who you are. For me, that moment happened not too long ago. I begin this book by sharing a story that has propelled my personal and professional life. I call this story "Chasing the 'Best.'" Even though sharing this tale with readers is not easy, I think it illustrates how many of us have felt for a long time. By starting this book with this story, I hope that we can set forth a pedagogy of play and hopeful transformation.

Chasing the "Best"

My life has long been guided by the profound need and intense desire to please my family, community, writing partners, daughters, friends, and professors so that they would accept me for who I am. Basically, I needed to please the world. For a long time, I felt small. Even my voice was small;

I spoke in a whisper. I wanted to be liked, so I compromised my being to please others. I believe this is something most of us tend to do. We follow, we agree, and we go along until something makes us realize that it is time to change.

Do you remember a time when you held back your voice, ideas, or desires so you would be accepted? Maybe when you were growing up, you wanted to blend in with the popular group in school. When we are continually looking for acceptance, we agree to many things we don't accept or want for ourselves. Perhaps now is the time to be the unique person you are and let your voice soar.

For me, it got to the point that no achievement was enough, and no success or award nurtured me enough. In my mind, I had not reached "the best." I lived with a constant pit in my stomach, an empty feeling I continuously needed to fill with unhealthy habits. I wanted the next best thing so badly because I wanted people to accept me and like me. I fell into despair, and I was emotionally wiped out. My life felt chaotic. I needed that acceptance so intensely that I sank lower and lower.

I became angry, and that anger manifested itself in unexpected moments. It was like an uncontrollable electrical charge. It burned me, and in the process, I burned others. It came out of blame, anxiety. It showed up in the destruction of my creativity and a feeling of profound desperation. I craved what other people had and wanted to be them. I imitated them and worked hard at it because, in my eyes, they were the best, better than me. However, it did not feel right. So, I leaped into presenting myself as larger than life, showing everyone that I was the expert who knew it all. Yet that did not feel any better. I was not showing my capacity for loving, caring, and giving. I stood tall but in anger. I saw the world as being out to get me. I took everything personally and became defensive. These emotions knocked me to my knees, and I cried in silence. I slept, ate, and basically self-destructed. I was in a chaotic pursuit to fulfill what everyone else told me was the best. I was not chasing *my* best.

In my worst moments, I often find solace in reading my favorite book, *The Little Prince* by Antoine de Saint-Exupéry. I read this book often, and every time I find golden nuggets of wisdom and guidance. During a low moment when I was reflecting on what I needed to do to change my perspective, this particular quote caught my attention, "All grown-ups were once children, but only a few remember it" (Saint-Exupéry 2019, Kindle location 64). The simple, wonderful quote raced through my every neuron.

I sprang out of my chair and said out loud, "I have been given a powerful gift, and it is time to use it." I had seen this gift in my observations of children playing and my research and writings, and I had come to realize it is one of the most powerful things humans have: our innate instinct and powerful urge to play. When children play, they find joy—the exhilaration of each moment of discovery and the laughter that comes from deep inside their bellies. They go into a flow where their passion and interests take over and nothing else matters.

I realized that I had lost my urge to play. Thus, I had lost my joy, my passion, and my creativity. After this revelation, I sent my mind to my fondest memories when I was joyful and creative. I remembered the days I spent in my jewelry shop, playing with metals and watching in fascination as the fire from the torch fused them together. I remembered how I used to freely play, not looking for perfectly measured jewelry. Instead, I allowed the fire and my creativity to determine the final product. I knew I needed to reclaim that feeling.

As I continued to look for ways to reconnect with my creative and playful spirit, I brought out a collection of Loose Parts and spent days just playing, just being present in the process. I was not looking to learn or to discover a hidden message. I just wanted to play. As I played, I let go of expectations, I let go of fear, and I became present in my whole being. I had reclaimed the playful side of my personality—that part of me that finds joy and humor in life.

So many of us adults have lost the power of play, and I fear that we will push children to lose it too if we do not reclaim it. Play has become an important part of my life, and my search to develop a playful attitude will continue to guide my journey to chase my best. Now I come to embrace daily moments of play, and I allow myself to be joyful and fully present. I am still chasing the best, except this time, I am pursuing my unapologetic whole best—a best grounded in courage, vulnerability, gratitude, and playfulness.

This book is timely because it comes when education is in disequilibrium and perhaps ready for sustainable change. Disequilibrium (that moment when what you know is challenged by new knowledge or information) is essential to the process of creativity and innovation because it pushes us to find new solutions and keeps us striving to find our passions and pursue our dreams. Disequilibrium propels us to ask questions without fixating on finding specific answers because new information sparks our curiosity and keeps our interest engaged. Fortunately, this disequilibrium can lead us to moments of powerful insight, the "aha!" moments that emerge with passion and creativity.

Throughout this book, I plan not only to engage you in reflection but also offer possibilities to reconnect to your childlike characteristics. The ensuing boost in creativity and innovation increases our support for children's right to play. This book offers a collection of tools, theories, ideas, and stories that I hope will support your efforts to play and rediscover your playful attitude. This book is designed to inspire and regenerate playfulness and creative leadership in all human beings who want to create a more playful pedagogy in their practices. They include educators, administrators, staff, community agencies, families, educational development companies, play therapists, educational franchise companies, coaches, directors of curriculum development and professional development, associations, and public and private educational entities.

The first chapters cover the research on adult play. I define the characteristics of play and the different play archetypes. I set a framework to deepen our understanding of adult play to help us create play ecosystems and change the culture of our organizations.

The second part of the book offers practical ideas you can implement in your organization. We start with redefining professional development to make it more playful while engaging staff in discovering their childhood genius. I walk you through steps to redesign the adult spaces in your program to elicit more play and playfulness. I then highlight a number of explorations and invitations to play both outdoors and indoors. I also offer ideas to rethink professional development conferences to break from the existing approach and increase opportunities to play and find joy.

Throughout the book, I remind us that play and playfulness are not forced or imposed. Instead, they require the thoughtful and intentional designing of a culture that embraces play and playfulness and invites people to find their whole "best."

CHAPTER 1

A Call to Just Play!

We don't stop playing because we grow old;
we grow old because we stop playing.

—attributed to George Bernard Shaw

I want to share the gift of playfulness with you. I want to share the power of play so that you can give it to children and to others. I want you to chase your best and let go of expectations that say you need to fulfill outcomes dictated by society. I hope you can learn to trust that inner you. Most important, I want you to recapture your childhood genius. And I want you to give children the gift of play so that they can discover their passion and hidden genius. Children know their own best, and the role of adults is to trust that knowledge. But before we can allow children to be their best, we must find our own best selves in all its definitions, manifestations, and representations.

I ask:

- Are we pushing ourselves and our children to chase "the best" that is imposed on them?

- What are the long-term repercussions of that constant external push for the best?

- Can we change our perspective and accept the authentic best in ourselves and in each child?

As I started to explore the idea of bringing play back into adulthood, I came across the concept of *neoteny*, or the retention of childlike behaviors into adulthood. Neoteny allows an adult to grow young by nurturing qualities that maintain playfulness and youthfulness. When we are growing up, we want to shed our childlike behaviors and embrace a grown-up attitude. Perhaps this desire to morph is derived from our need and want to be accepted. In the book *Growing Young*, author Ashley Montagu discusses the significance of neoteny in our social development and retaining juvenile physical characteristics into adulthood: "When this process is carried over from physical traits to behavioral patterns, human beings can revolutionize their lives and become for the first time, perhaps, the kinds of creatures their heritage has prepared them to be—youthful all the days of their lives" (Montagu 1989, Kindle locations 75–77).

When we observe children, we see some characteristics that as adults we should aspire to embrace. Curiosity is high on this list because it leads to positive change through innovation, imaginativeness, playfulness, open-mindedness, willingness to experiment, flexibility, humor, energy, receptiveness to new ideas, honesty, eagerness to learn, and, perhaps the most pervasive and valuable of all, the need to love (Montagu 1989).

Play is crucial in adulthood because it fosters adaptiveness, creativity, role rehearsal (trying out new roles or possible careers), and mind-body integration. When adults engage in play and creative endeavors, they find their childlike center that cultivates happiness and joy. Play is affirming because it allows us to enter a natural, safe, and caring environment where we freely explore our inner thinking and desires. For example, I enjoy dressing up in different period costumes. I have created a persona that represents my personality but also challenges me and allows other traits to emerge. When I role-play, I begin to make sense of moments I am facing in my real life and I find more flexibility in my decision-making. Being in a playful and inspired flow, such as when we dance or engage in some sort of creative activity, allows us to cultivate happiness and joy. We discover new ways to make meaning in the world, and we also realize how liberating it is to let go of constraints.

If you ask me how I learned that play is essential, I could not give you a single answer. I went to college to learn about human development and counseling. I studied under renowned scholars and grew my practice with incredible mentors, and I am still not sure that I can tell you how I learned to value play. I have seen many children (including my own) engaged in play, laughing and existing entirely in the creative flow. It got me closer to an answer, but I still can't say this is how I learned that play is essential. That's probably because the answer is multifaceted, and sometimes we are confused by play's complexity.

Here is what I do know . . .

Because we create our own identities, each of us is unique in the way we approach play and learning. No single perfect answer or experience validates what we know. Only an inquisitive attitude allows us to see things from multiple perspectives. We play to be, perhaps to explore the possibilities of being someone different. We play to dream about who we will become. We play because it is transformational. We learn from play because our hearts, souls, and minds are open to diverse perspectives and realities. When we play as adults, we are able to see children for their unique way of being in the world.

I also know . . .

The images we see daily (in art, advertising, or symbols) require us to reflect on our experiences and the ever-changing nature of our perceptions. When we see a work of art, we have to carefully analyze our reactions, emotions, and perceptions to give meaning to what we have seen. The same happens when we observe children or adults at play. However, what is essential is that we value play as freedom and liberation from societal constraints. Play and learning happen as we explore, connect, and reflect on our experiences. When we explore and connect with the experience (the materials, the people, the space), free of mandates and standards, we become more curious and intentional in everything we do.

I am learning that . . .

Transformation happens in a community when we know that we belong. When we play and learn in relationships, we discover our strengths, open our minds to new possibilities, and cocreate new realities and more hopeful futures. In play we engage in relationships that both value and invite our contribution. We often talk about socializing children and designing programs that we believe will make them more accepted by society at large. I have learned that programs and strategies are not enough to help children develop social skills. We also need to create a community where everyone's contribution is valued and we can share in the joy of having meaningful relationships.

I have learned the meaning of practice . . .

In practice we make room for mistakes to be celebrated and revisited. When we practice, we find what we are capable of and what we need to change. When we see play and learning as freedom, we create ecosystems that allow us to practice and test our theories. Play and learning are about *praxis*, or taking a hypothesis through prototyping, testing, discovering, and redesigning. Play and learning happen in the process, not when we focus on outcomes. I believe that results will not occur until we engage in the process of play and learning.

I know that we must redefine the meaning of *learning* to move away from simplistic approaches, such as teaching the ABCs and 123s or prescribing specific thematic concepts. Instead, we need to implement an education that liberates the power of creativity and joy.

I also know that when adults play, we become more inspired to promote the value of play. We understand more deeply how it is a central part of our humanity. Play is not a luxury; it's a basic need that we must ensure is available to all. That is why we must change our professional development to embrace the power of play.

However, we must acknowledge differences in children's and adults' perceptions and play needs. Children play instinctively, while adults make a conscious choice to play. As adults, we often have time constraints and prefer to schedule specific times to play, precluding more spontaneous types of play. We adults may be reluctant to engage in play wholeheartedly in front of other adults for fear of being ridiculed. Encouraging other adults to play requires us to consider how they will make a choice to play and how they will stay engaged, so appreciating the distinction between child and adult play is crucial when designing play spaces for adults. Play for adults has to remove barriers by creating a trusting space where people are free to play and be silly without the fear of being ridiculed. Creating playful spaces requires leaders to remove distractions, such as worksheets and limiting activities for teaching academic content, that drag the focus toward assessments and teaching pedagogies.

I know this seems challenging, but it is a worthy effort because reclaiming joy and playfulness will go a long way toward reclaiming creativity and higher learning in both adults and children. As an educational leader, I often invite adults to play. I offer different opportunities to be creative, such as exploring paint, sculpting with clay, playing with words, or engaging in dance and movement. As difficult as it may be to first engage in play, with a variety of opportunities everyone can find one that feels comfortable and inviting.

Just Play!

Today's educators are working harder than ever, putting in long hours, drowning in never-ending paperwork, and reaching the point of hopelessness and burnout. Pressures are ramping up for educators to meet performance standards that demand greater efficiency, quicker returns, and more accountability than in years past. Unfortunately, many educational systems are not providing the level of support educators need. The consistent expectation to adapt to ongoing change combined with low wages has caused many creative educators to leave the profession to find perhaps less satisfying but more financially rewarding jobs.

As educators, we are also experiencing an identity crisis. We continue working hard to gain recognition for the work we do and to achieve higher compensation. Yet in a misguided attempt to increase student "achievement," we are also constantly pushed to join in practices (such as testing children for content knowledge) that compromise the values we hold close to our hearts: such as playfulness, joy, creativity, empathy, community, and compassion. We want professional recognition, but we also want to advocate for what we know is best for young children. We want to embrace our creativity and adopt the pedagogies of play and care, which we understand have the power to sustain and change children's lives.

As a profession, we must regain our identity and focus on what we know brings joy to children, families, and communities. We must recognize that every interaction with young children is powerful and filled with teaching and learning exchanges. It is time to regenerate our profession and end the identity crisis collectively. We do not need to define education as the process of memorizing the word of the week or reciting components of the calendar. Instead, we must reclaim the privilege of giving children a love for nature, Loose Parts, clay, art, construction, sand, water, and mud. Let's find the joy of moving, singing, rhyming, and engaging in imaginative play. Let's create fantasy worlds that stretch our creativity. Let's connect and build friendships and meaningful relationships. We must invent a new language that describes the pedagogies of play and of care and that starts to redefine what teaching and learning are about so that we can protect, honor, and respect the culture of childhood. We must lean in and just play to create a playful culture where educators can freely bring their best to work.

To engage playfulness, creativity, and innovation, ecosystems must do the following:

- Free up time from the pursuit of predictable goals to engage curiosity and look for surprises. Shift meetings from task-oriented processes to more playful engagement and collective idea making. Instead of just discussing required outcomes, harness the power of the brainstorm and hive mind or sketch and represent ideas using Loose Parts. Try exploring "the worst possible idea" presented and find the most creative solutions. Play with words, play with art, play with blocks. In other words, find solutions in a playful process.

- Work with the body's natural circadian rhythms, which affect our emotions and behaviors. Knowing when we need to rest, play, or work can help us discover at which times we are more productive individually and as an ecosystem. If most of the educators in the ecosystem function with more energy in the morning and they seem to be less creative in the afternoons, shift the meeting times. Redesign the temporal schedule of the ecosystem to better help children and educators find a more engaging and productive rhythm. Begin by scheduling longer unbroken times to play in the morning and later in the afternoon. After all, when we are more energetic, we are more open to exploring new ideas.

- Create spaces and places that enhance reflective thought, playfulness, and creativity. For example, introduce a new medium to explore at every meeting and reflect on how the medium helps develop creativity. I often use photographs and paint over them, or draw on them using a tablet or tracing light table. Since I do not have the most developed drawing ability, the photos give me the freedom to explore my creativity in a different way or use a medium I have not explored before.

- Invite people to work in groups to promote innovation, break away from familiar structures, and introduce greater playfulness into the ecosystem. Have everyone wear disposable painter's coveralls and use permanent markers to write their ideas on one another's backs. Then display the coveralls. When I do this fun activity, the laughter fuels people's creativity, and the ideas that surface are often worth pursuing.

- Go beyond merely listening to new ideas to prototyping them and producing an inexpensive, scaled-down example. Prototyping gives educators the opportunity to test ideas' practicality. The rest of the team can offer suggestions to modify the design or discard the idea before it is fully implemented. For example, when an idea to modify the physical space emerges, people can play together to create a scaled-down mock-up using cardboard and other materials before they make changes to the actual space.

- Transcend restrictive routines and instead create invitations to play. Change the schedule and plan for more time to play together as a team.

- Laugh together, share humor, and give one another the freedom to embrace authenticity. Accept one another with care and compassion.

The more people embrace playfulness, the more they will be creative contributors to the ecosystem. When people embrace the positive mood associated with playfulness, they become more open to new ideas and change.

Remember that when faced with uncertainty at work, people can watch and helplessly let changes happen, or they can do something by actively trying to create the future they want. I invite you to join the groups of people who embrace the change, instability, complexity, and discomfort that come from confusing and unpredictable circumstances. These educators believe it is possible to thrive in the chaos brought by change. They are professionals who turn challenging situations to their advantage and find elements of stability and contentment in their endeavors. They succeed because they have found time to play and rekindle their creativity. They grow because they embrace playfulness and lean into tension. They understand that disequilibrium and tension indicate when we are entering a period of learning and sustainable change. Playful educators are open to being in a state of wonder, which means that they are more open and creative, able to hear both their own wisdom and the wisdom of others.

The Tenets of Play

I propose the following tenets to help us shift from focusing on performance at work to a more playful and fun attitude. These can be adopted by individuals, programs, organizations, or anyone who wants to create a playful culture in their work ecosystems.

TENET 1: Bring your own best to the ecosystem. Share who you are and open your heart and soul to learn about others' best too.

● JUST PLAY! CHALLENGE ●

Invite people to define and share their own best by using different art media or Loose Parts to create representational art showing their experience. This can be an ongoing and ever-changing play experience.

Ask yourself: How did I feel when I defined my best and had an opportunity to represent it? How might I continue to chase my best instead of chasing the best others have defined for me?

TENET 2: Be honest about your own perceptions of work and play. Reflect on how this perception affects your well-being and that of the children you care for and educate.

JUST PLAY! CHALLENGE

- Play with words and play with objects.

- Use Loose Parts to show you're thinking about play.

- Write a poem explaining how play is different from work.

- Document your play experiences with photography.

Ask yourself: How does the play inform and transform my practices?

TENET 3: Trust the process and let go of the need for children to obtain specific educational outcomes. Embrace a culture of disequilibrium and change. It is within this disequilibrium that we enter more fulfilling learning.

JUST PLAY! CHALLENGE

For every time that the O word (outcomes) comes into your mind, engage in unscripted play. After at least fifteen minutes of play, identify how many outcomes have been met.

TENET 4: Dare to laugh, play, and be spontaneous. Find comfort in play, and invent opportunities to bring laughter into your work. Don't plan every moment of the day, whether it is your workday or your own personal life. Let go of plans and instead invite spontaneity.

JUST PLAY! CHALLENGE

Take the time to share a joke with a friend, see a funny movie, or be spontaneous and do something fun that you have been waiting to do for a long time.

TENET 5: Engage in play and discussions that include diverse perspectives. Let go of the idea of "agreeing to disagree," which to me means that everyone still holds on to their own opinions and continues to act the same as before, with no solution or willingness to explore ideas that could benefit both parties. It is a stance based on the belief "I am right, and I will not change." Instead, make room for all ideas and voices. Learn to listen and find common ground that can further support the relationship. Be open to dialogue, and listen by giving your full attention. Embrace your compassion and make every effort to understand one another's perspectives and negotiate until you achieve a clear understanding of your common goal.

● JUST PLAY! CHALLENGE ●

Next time you find yourself in a conversation where there is no agreement, discuss how it feels to win and lose. Can the win-or-lose be changed into a game that builds understanding rather than an agreement? Find solutions together.

Play a game of solving the conflict for the common good. Start with a situation, and then explore the conflict without finding a single winner. For example, say there is just one lemon left and each person wants to use it differently. Someone wants to make juice, another wants to cook with it, and a third person would rather use it in baking. They can't agree on who gets to keep the lemon. Instead of one person negotiating to win the lemon, each person needs to come up with an alternative solution that benefits everyone. Perhaps the first thing they realize is that one lemon is not enough for a large project, but each person could get a slice to flavor a glass of water.

TENET 6: Renegotiate rules and expand boundaries. When rules lead your work and practices, they can constrict creativity. Reflect on expanding the boundaries to make room for different ideas. Question the rules and decide whether they are too restrictive or even necessary.

● JUST PLAY! CHALLENGE ●

Select a game to play. Before you start, discuss the rules of the game written in the manual. Discuss each rule and analyze how it might affect the creativity of playing the game. Change the rules or get rid of them altogether. Now play the game and see how people relax and enjoy themselves. This conversation can then be used to analyze each of the rules that guide your practices in your program.

TENET 7: Bring your authenticity with you. Let people know your playful side without fear of being ostracized or criticized.

● JUST PLAY! CHALLENGE ●

Play every day. Play alone and play in groups. Authenticity will grow, and all will feel more comfortable and relaxed. Play will help you find the *me* while joining the *we*.

Ask yourself: How do I feel as I play? How does play support my relationships?

TENET 8: Shift your perspective from a "doing" state of mind to a more "being" in the moment state of mind. Be present and stop worrying about meeting standards. Listen, smell, and breathe every day. Connect to the laughter of children and be joyful. Find your authentic playful attitude.

● JUST PLAY! CHALLENGE ●

Play "Guess Whose List It Is." To-do lists take the characteristics of their owners. Some are perfectly written and color-coded. Some are messy and hand-written. Others look like life is spilling over the edges. Some have emojis and a lot of punctuation reminders. Collect to-do lists from the participants in advance. Redact names and words that make the writers' identity obvious, and then pass the lists around without saying who wrote them. Everyone tries to match the list to the person who wrote it. Extend the game by asking people to add an idea for fun to each person's list.

TENET 9: Give yourself permission to do what you love doing. Playfulness is a choice; you can choose to bring the best of your whole self to work every day.

● JUST PLAY! CHALLENGE ●

Make a box with permission slips. Have people write one another permission to do something playful each day or when stress takes over. The cards serve as a reminder that it is okay to be playful and silly.

Example: I give Miriam permission to make jewelry for at least thirty minutes today.

TENET 10: Invite risk-taking. To be a successful risk-taker means overcoming our fear of failure and embracing mistakes and mishaps. Create opportunities to take risks and reflect on how fear has limited your playful attitude.

● JUST PLAY! CHALLENGE ●

Challenge one another to take a risk and let go of finding a correct answer. Write a risk you will be taking today. When a "wrong" or "I can't" thought comes into your head, rewrite it as a possibility for further risk-taking.

TENET 11: Embrace learning to learn. Remember that *what* we learn is not as important as the learning process itself. The most important gift we can give ourselves and children is learning how to learn. This requires us to let go of finding correct answers and instead develop a profound interest in learning to learn. Learning to learn requires us to play with different strategies and not just memorize a simple answer or fact. Different challenges need new approaches, since doing the same thing every time won't lead to sustainable change.

● JUST PLAY! CHALLENGE ●

Play a strategy game. A strategy game reminds us that everything we do requires planning, creativity, and innovation. I often play the strategic board game Settlers of Catan. It is engaging and requires thinking. It also promotes conversations about strategy and problem solving.

Play an ongoing collective game of trivia. When you do not know the answer, invite others to come up with the answer. After all, you do not always have to be the only person to come up with the "right" answer. This challenge creates a collective synergy.

Ask yourself: What is it like to find answers and solutions from other people and not always have to be the holder of knowledge?

TENET 12: Celebrate both mistakes and successes. Integrate celebration into everyday life. Dance, clap, and give high fives when people discover something new or accomplish a goal. Just as important, learn to celebrate mistakes as opportunities for change and growth.

● JUST PLAY! CHALLENGE ●

- Play to celebrate the micro-achievements and mistakes we make each day. We learn from both.

- Keep a basket with all you need to play simple childhood games: marbles, jacks, jump rope, sidewalk chalk for art or hopscotch, pickup sticks, string for cat's cradle, a yo-yo, and a top, to name a few. Add this sign to the basket: "Don't forget to play today!"

Reflections

- When you enter moments of disequilibrium, what will you do to allow your curiosity to guide your learning?

- Which of the tenets resonate with you most? Why?

- What steps will you take to incorporate the tenets of play and playfulness into your ecosystem?

- What strategies will you use to embrace change?

CHAPTER 2

The Power of Adult Play

In play we transform the world according to our
desires, while in learning, we transform ourselves
better to conform to the structure of the world.

—Jerome Bruner

The word *play* may seem deceptively simple to define, but when we search
for its meaning we find a wide range of answers from personal experiences
and research. We may hear, "Play is the work of children" or "Play is different from work." So what does that mean, and how do the ideas of play and
work guide our thinking? Comparing play to work seems to take away the
power of play for the sake of play. Do we always have to make everything
seem like work? I propose that play is for the purpose of pleasure! Yes, play
can enhance our work life, but play should not be considered work, even
for young children.

What we do know to be true is that every ounce of learning derives from play. This is why we must understand what play is and communicate our understanding to families and colleagues. Before we can advocate for play, we must develop a clear construct of its meaning, and we can only develop our mental construct by immersing ourselves in play. Until we experience play ourselves as adults, it is difficult to define it or to facilitate it for young children.

When we play, we enter into a state of flow, as described by Mihaly Csikszentmihalyi (1997)—the flow that comes when you are fully immersed in a pleasurable and intriguing process. Being in a state of flow brings a highly focused level of consciousness that promotes innovation. When we are playful, we can think flexibly, take risks with ideas, and allow our creative thoughts to emerge. Play has its own intrinsic rewards. We know that at the heart of play is the pleasure of engaging in the activity or thought process for its own sake, without the expectation of being rewarded or recognized. But play can bring material rewards too, for instance, when we see the outcomes of successful innovation that benefits colleagues, children, and families.

There is a difference between *play* and *playfulness*. Play is an action. More specifically, it is based in a moment when we are focused on a specific action, such as when we engage in dramatic play. Play is the act of building a block structure for the purpose of accomplishing an idea or pursuing a theory. The focus is on the play, or act of building. Playfulness is a state of mind that leads to wonder, discovery, flexible thinking, and risk-taking. Playfulness requires vulnerability and openness to the unknown. Playfulness allows us to enjoy watching the block tower fall without feeling that our hard work is destroyed.

Play is an approach to activity and is focused on the actions themselves. It is a holistic experience that invites our total being into the process. You are fully focused on the action of play. Playfulness is when you bring actions of play, such as joy, fun, or humor, to an activity that is not pure play. A playful activity has the purpose beyond playing for its own sake. Playfulness becomes a personality trait and cognitive style, influencing who we are and how we understand the world. In early childhood education, we need both play and playfulness.

People may have their own definitions of *play* and *playfulness*. What you consider to be playful may not be to the next person. But we do not have to worry if what we are doing is considered play as long as we embrace a playful mindset. What is important is that we are free, relaxed, happy, and flowing, instead of constantly checking our watch to see when we must stop our play. Given the opportunity, each of us will find a definition of *play* that makes sense to us. We do not necessarily need to play to be playful. We just need to be present and yield to the moment, ready to respond to new opportunities. I use the following "playful" framework when I prepare to engage people in play:

- **P**resent: We are present and in the moment, and we find a sense of place and belonging.

- **L**asting: We construct lasting memories that sustain us for the rest of our lives.

- **A**ffinity: We build relationships with people and the environment.

- **Y**ou: We focus on ourselves to find our childhood genius.

- **F**low: We are fully immersed in what we are doing. When we are in a state of flow, we achieve greater enjoyment, energy, creativity, and involvement.

- **U**nity: The mind, heart, body, and soul become one entity.

- **L**earning: We learn for the passion and joy of it.

Creating a playful culture is more than play; it is about being aware of our playfulness and passion for play. It requires us to be keenly aware of when we are playful and when we are not. Playfulness comes from the center of who we are—our mind, heart, body, and soul. While the research on the benefits of adult play is minimal, and it often focuses on the therapeutic value of play rather than play for the sole purpose of enjoyment, still we can find myriad reasons why play improves lives.

Play Is Essential to Human Behavior

Research is robust about the importance of play in promoting healthy child development. In the book *Play: Its Role in Development and Evolution*, Jerome Bruner, Alison Jolly, and Kathy Sylva analyze the influence of play on the development of children and primates. They take a close look at the conditions that promote play and the role of the adult in play (Bruner, Sylva, and Jolly 1985). In his book *The Genesis of Animal Play: Testing the Limits*, professor of psychology Gordon Burghardt argues that playfulness may be essential to be human. He states that playfulness develops through a specific set of interactions among developmental, evolutionary, ecological, and physiological processes (Burghardt 2006). Burghardt also offers working definitions of play by setting out five categorical criteria for recognizing play in all species, including humans. I find the following criteria helpful in the context of this book:

CRITERION 1: We do not need play to survive. From this I extrapolate that the purpose of play is enjoyment. Although play is not necessary for individual survival, it promotes creativity and innovation and the attainment of survival goals, and I believe that it is essential for the survival of the soul of humanity. I cannot prove this point, but I do know how I feel when days go by and I do not play. I begin to feel isolation and sadness, an intense pain inside similar to hunger pangs.

CRITERION 2: Play is voluntary, spontaneous, intentional, pleasurable, rewarding, reinforcing, and autotelic ("done for its own sake"). In other words, play and perhaps playfulness is a choice and a way of life. Human beings, like animals, have an innate need to play, and providing them opportunities to choose to play will contribute to a more rewarding life.

CRITERION 3: Play differs from "serious" activities structurally and temporally, as play can be left incomplete, players can exaggerate it, and it is often undervalued by those involved. Play has its own timeline and space in which it defines its path and meaning. We habitually consider play in contrast to work, but this dilutes play's value because it is not an incomplete or limited "work" but is valuable in its own right and is crucial to the full development of humans throughout their lifespan. However, although an activity such as a game might lack seriousness, the immersive engagement of players in the game can make it feel serious and important.

CRITERION 4: Play can be repetitive and flexible. Because we enjoy playing so much, we want to continue to play and repeat the same process until we are fully satisfied with the outcome or solution. Like children, adults must play and revisit experiences to make meaning and explore solutions to situations.

CRITERION 5: Play happens when we are adequately fed, healthy, and free from stress or intense competing systems. In other words, play exists once basic human needs are met. Yet I would argue that play is so essential to fulfillment and self-actualization that it coexists with basic survival needs, and thus we need to feed it with excitement and joy.

● JUST PLAY! CHALLENGE ●

Go on a photographic safari searching for play in the "wild." Take photos of children fully immersed in play. Play around with the moments you capture in the photographs, for example:

● Re-create the play you captured in the photograph. If it is dramatic play, wear the costumes and explore what the child felt and did, or simply engage in your own sequence of dramatic play.

● If the children were playing a game, invite your colleagues to play the same game, or invent a new game together.

● Try art explorations of what you see in the photographs. Play with an art medium you have not fully explored before.

● Reflect with others on what story the photos tell you and what you learned from your play. Discuss each of the five criteria of play and how each can be supported in your daily life.

Play and Playfulness Rekindle Creativity

Throughout human history, people have believed that creativity is an inherently mysterious and impenetrable biological gift, and you have "it" or you don't. As a result, we cling to a series of false myths about what creativity is and how it develops. These myths don't just mislead—they interfere with creativity. For the past thirty years in my work as an early childhood educator and professor, I have noticed that many college students do not see themselves as creative humans. They resist change, as they fear doing things differently or confronting perceived limitations in their abilities and capacities. Caught within the parameters of fear and lacking trust in their own powers, they have found support in boxed curricula, worksheets, and crafts they can copy. When they feel more adventurous, they scroll through Pinterest to find inspiration they can duplicate. I argue that when educators do not engage their own creativity, in turn they do not support children's creativity, negatively affecting their development.

Today's educational systems have lost their creative backbone. More and more educators, administrators, and families are demanding a standardized educational system that leaves behind creativity and innovation. Current educational practices have a narrow focus on academics and have failed to support the complex systems through which children learn. It is time to shift the paradigm and help education become a system where play, creativity, and innovation are embraced. The educational and developmental theories that have influenced the early childhood profession emphasize how spontaneity and freedom are essential characteristics in play because they influence the growing individual's emotional, social, and intellectual development.

Playfulness is linked to creativity and innovative thinking. Creative people tend to be more open to new ideas and apply divergent thinking in their work. Tim Brown, CEO of the design firm IDEO, explained this pragmatic side to playfulness. In his video presentation, Brown (2008, 7:59) states, "We think playfulness helps us to get better solutions. It helps us do our jobs better and helps us feel better when we do them." When we embrace play and playfulness, we also engage in more fluid, flexible, and imaginative thinking. Fluency in play refers to the number of different ideas generated when a person is asked about alternative uses for a particular object. Flexibility refers to the capacity to switch between approaches and generate ideas from different sources (Bateson and Martin 2015). Imaginative thinking refers to the ability to envision a bright future.

As we move onward in the twenty-first century, society requires creativity and imagination to sustain innovation and change. As educators, we are called to prepare children to work in the unknown future, so there is nothing more compelling than reconnecting to our creativity and playfulness and, together with children, having the freedom to imagine a successful future.

Too often as adults we are concerned about other people's judgment. We feel embarrassed about sharing our ideas and fear rejection and criticism. But these feelings are a barrier to creative and innovative thinking. Robert H. McKim, professor emeritus at Stanford's School of Design, developed a simple test to demonstrate how these feelings of inadequacy stunt our creative spirit. In your next meeting, ask people to draw a portrait of the person sitting next to them. Give them thirty seconds to complete the portrait. You will probably hear laughter and a sense of uncomfortableness. If you ask them to share their masterpieces, you will probably experience hesitation and reluctance. Contrary to children, who proudly share their work, adults have been subjected to opinions and criticism and often are more reluctant to share their creative ideas. This is why we must create ecosystems where play is valued for both adults and children—so that people feel safe and can engage their more creative selves.

Imagine coming to work with the expectation that your ideas and creative innovations will be valued and expected. Think of walking into an ecosystem that sends the message that you are here to play and be creative. The hard work of being an educator becomes joyful and engaging. When the workplace values creativity and innovation and play is integrated into every aspect of the ecosystem, we help people become more comfortable with showing their playful attitudes. I often break through people's reluctance by leading an exploration of one tool or one material at a time. I stress that process leads to successful outcomes. When we focus on meeting outcomes instead of letting the process guide us, we are less willing to explore our creativity.

In 2020 during the COVID-19 pandemic, we saw many adults searching for opportunities to be creative: During 2020 there was an increase in sales of adult coloring books and coloring supplies. (Personally, I bought almost every art media I could find!) Many children's parks and recreation centers are scheduling adult playtime. Businesses are hiring play experts to engage employees in play explorations that increase creativity. In other words, we are beginning to recognize adults' need to play. Is it not time that the early childhood education ecosystem shifted to embrace adult play and playfulness?

When you tackle a complex challenge, you need a group of people wired with creativity and ready to provide innovative solutions. Hackathons are events at which participants design and pitch an innovative solution to a challenge. This concept originated in the tech world and is often used to create new apps and products. However, you can use a hackathon to engage educators in solving challenges in creative ways. Begin by dividing people into small groups. Give them a theme without providing a lot of information on the challenge.

Theme examples include:

● Build more time for collaborative reflection and planning.

● Create an inclusive, equitable, and authentic community.

● Design a system to complete required observations and paperwork.

You can also ask people to give you their most overwhelming challenges in advance to use as themes. It is essential to focus on one challenge at a time.

Once you have a theme, participants enter the hackathon to design the most elegant solution to the challenge.

The solution includes:

Define: Describe the challenge, the process, and the value.

Design: Create a prototype that can be easily used and implemented. For this part of the process, incorporate many tools to play with. Educators can use role play, construction, art, Loose Parts, and so on. The point is to engage in a creative process as they test their ideas.

Discover: Use photographs, recordings, and narrative stories to help gather the data and story of what you do.

Once the groups complete their solutions, each team pitches their idea to the large group. As a group, a decision is made about the solution that can be further developed, implemented, and tested.

What is valuable about a hackathon is the infusion of creativity. Everyone is focused on finding the optimal solution to a problem and is ready to tackle the answer together.

Play and Playfulness
Support Equity and Inclusion

Play is central in building community, enhancing education, and trans-forming lives, which together can lead to authentic equity and a more civil society. When adults gather to play, they engage in equitable and inclusive practices that sustain their work and life. In play every voice is heard, and every voice has its purpose and value. When we intentionally plan to cre-ate a playful culture, the design and facilitation of meetings, gatherings, planning, policies, and interactions use an equity and inclusion lens. When adults play together, they are part of equity-centered ecosystems. The eco-systems in turn support their members through sustainable change. In play we build bridges to eliminate inequalities rooted in race, ethnicity, gender, sexual orientation, differences of ability, social class, language, geo-graphical location, religion, and all other characteristics.

Humans are born curious. We are inspired to learn, master new skills, and cultivate talents with agency and resiliency. It is also clear that a lack of play can crush the human spirit. Our creativity is diminished to the point that we stop caring and reject growth and change outright, feel apathetic or alienated, or give up on making responsible contributions to society. This includes educators who go through the motions of teaching or make deci-sions that adversely affect children (Ryan and Deci 2000). Unfortunately, when trying to meet unforgiving performance standards, well-meaning educators can focus too much on these expectations instead of the children themselves. For example, this may happen when a child is not sitting still and listening or completing an adult-led activity and the teacher removes the child instead of changing the way the activity is conducted. When a teacher harshly prevents children from participating, they receive the mes-sage that they are not capable, which harms the children and blocks social and emotional learning in the situation. When educators have a playful attitude, these moments often can be shifted to a more positive outcome. This is especially important for children in historically excluded and under-funded communities, including Black and brown children, particularly boys, who are disciplined more harshly for their behavior. According to Yale researcher Walter S. Gilliam and colleagues, inherent teacher bias leads to a disproportionate number of Black and brown boys being sus-pended in preschool (Gilliam et al. 2016). I venture to say that creating a more playful culture can prevent these negative biases from filtering into the early childhood ecosystems. When educators gain in understanding and address their inherent biases, they build the empathy that can prevent expulsions and harsh punishment.

Being playful makes us more patient, proactive, and persistent because we reclaim our childhood genius, encompassing flexibility, inventiveness, creativity, and joy. Both adults and children desire to be free to make decisions, learn, and exercise power over personal choices. We want to know that we belong and that our contributions are accepted and valued. We have a profound desire to accomplish our goals and feel successful in our work. There is no better vehicle to reclaim authenticity, equity, and inclusion than full and wholehearted engagement in play.

We create the following when we play together:

- **Equity of voice:** We listen to one other, we value diverse perspectives, and we coexist within our unique ways of being in the world. When we are playful, we stop taking everything that is said so personally, so trust can develop.

- **Inclusion:** We can play in different ways and participate with freedom.

- **Collective perspectives:** Our play contributes to the group and helps us learn collectively.

Play and Playfulness
Build Relationships

Playfulness supports relationship building because it requires a complete openness toward one another. When we play together, we increase the level of connection we have with others. When adults play together, they rekindle joy and excitement and build resiliency. Play helps people get over grudges, resentments, and pain. In play, adults rediscover a more authentic way of being and see the power of diverse perspectives. Through play, we learn to trust one another, creating safe and brave spaces where we can laugh, listen to one another, and find common ground. Trust enables us to work together, open ourselves to intimacy, and try new things. By making a conscious effort to incorporate more humor and play into our daily interactions, we can improve the quality of love relationships as well as our connections with coworkers, family members, and friends.

Social skills develop and improve as part of the give-and-take of play. During childhood play, kids learn about verbal communication, body language, boundaries, cooperation, and teamwork. As adults, we continue to refine these skills through play and playful communication. Through play, we learn to work together, follow mutually agreed-upon rules, and socialize in groups. As adults, we can continue to use play to break down barriers. Incorporating play ecosystems into the workplace increases adults' joyfulness and their willingness to fully participate in sustaining and regenerating the creative impetus of the organization.

One of the reasons adults play is to connect with others and reclaim their social well-being. We join groups based on our interests, seek the company of like-minded people, play board games, or join sports leagues. We look for healthy after-work play outlets and forms of recreation, and we also enjoy team-building exercises at work. Playing is how we connect to people.

Play and Playfulness
Encourage Collaboration

What childhood memories do you have of playing? I remember organizing games to solve a problem or accomplish a specific goal. The excitement of the moment brought us together, and we stayed focused to devise solutions. In the book *Roxaboxen* by Alice McLerran, children gather every summer to build an imaginary city, working together to create homes, stores, and other dwellings. Their play goes on for years, and they negotiate and collaborate to accomplish their common goal.

Many of us adults have memories of negotiating rules during play when we were children. We can use these memories as a starting point to encourage us to play together and learn from one another. Play automatically improves social skills and interaction with others, whether children, families, or colleagues are participating. Playing together promotes a sense of belonging and community. Building bonds at work can also build a positive foundation to encourage business and develop strong relationships with stakeholders. Fun, by definition, makes people happy, and happy people are more productive.

Playing games together enhances collaboration. Setting up a culture of play that encourages collaborative and collegial games can increase bonding and creativity. I recently gathered with the NOW (Neighbors of Wine, a happy hour group that meets weekly) to play the word game Quiddler. Rather than a competition, it became a collaborative game, and we amused ourselves helping one another come up with the most creative words.

When people get to know one another and like one another, they are more willing to work together. Encouraging activities that help people bond personally and socially can go a long way in supporting collaboration. The best method I have found is through play.

Play and Playfulness Generate Energy and Synergy

I have clear memories of the days after the terrorist attacks of September 11, 2001. My yearning to find joy and hope led me to the children at the child development center on the college campus where I taught. Listening to their laughter energized me and allowed me to bring that energy to my students. I shifted from lecturing to designing playful explorations. We painted, sculpted, played games, listened to music, told stories, and danced. The energy was palpable, and the learning surpassed my expectations. At that moment, I realized adults need as much play as children.

When we adopt a playful outlook and lead a life with humor and playfulness, we are free from regret about the past or fear of the future. Incorporating more humor, fun, and play into everyday interactions can improve our energy and prevent burnout. That uplifting feeling remains with us even after the laughter has subsided. Play and laughter energize us, help us develop an optimistic outlook, and allow us to address loss and disappointment with strength. Like laughter, energy is contagious. When we spend time with an energetic person, we can't help but feel energetic and ready to tackle difficult tasks. We all have memories of walking into work and being surrounded by the energy children exude. When we join in their play and laughter, our energy becomes propulsion for enjoyment. To have an energetic workforce, we must center our ecosystems on play, playfulness, and joy.

Playfulness happens in spaces that connect a sense of belonging with a sense of wonder. Playful ecosystems emerge when play and playfulness bring forward educators' creativity and passion. A culture where playful synergy exists recognizes that play is essential to learning and frees people to play, laugh, and be joyful.

This idea of creating a playful culture motivated me to write this book. I have a profound desire to create play ecosystems because I believe that each one of us has the capacity to be playful at work and in life. We want people to feel the freedom to contribute and give back, resulting in a positive difference in the lives of children, families, and educators. If we nurture playfulness in early childhood educators and if leaders dare to be playful, as a society we will become happier, more inventive, and eventually more resilient and flexible.

Play and Playfulness Increase Critical Thinking

My mother was a brilliant and active person. She loved sudoku and playing poker. She had bursts of powerful and contagious laughter that pulled you into her world. In her last year of life, she struggled with Parkinson's disease. Sometimes the medication affected her and her brain was not as sharp. We brought her playing cards and puzzles to keep her mind active. Sometimes she would just move the cards around, not really playing a game but always pretending and with full concentration. Other times you would see her sharpness return as she engaged in a game of solitaire, smiling as she placed the cards in order. That brilliant smile reminded me of that creative person who found many ways to express her ideas and interests. Those playful moments that my mother found as she engaged in her favorite activities show in real life how we increase our critical-thinking abilities through play.

Critical thinking requires an agile and flexible mind. Successful people are critical and creative thinkers who can adapt different strategies to life circumstances and respond appropriately to make the most of the changes, decisions, and unexpected moments at the heart of life. Unfortunately, it's also quite human to develop thinking patterns that are based on misconceptions, biases, stereotypes, and distortions. But when we play and laugh together, we are more likely to dismantle misconceptions about one another *and* better understand a problem while solving it together.

When we have a playful attitude, we become more aware of our thoughts and intentions. Play also helps us adopt a collective mindset and create a new culture that serves a common purpose. Imagine having a culture at work that values thinking together as you engage in playful explorations that provide multiple answers to a single challenge. When people engage in play and develop a playful attitude, they gain a deeper perspective of how sustainable change can happen within an organization.

Play and Playfulness Relieve Stress

Sometimes stress slowly enters our lives. Once there, it tends to linger. At other times, life challenges, changes, and crises such as the COVID-19 pandemic confront us suddenly. People tell us to take the challenges one step at a time or send us motivational messages to keep us going. Sometimes these messages ease the stress, but other times they are merely empty words. In these moments, we should embrace the power of play. It brings laughter, relaxation, and understanding with much greater effectiveness than any platitude.

Playing is a healthy activity for adults as well as children. It reduces cortisol levels. High cortisol levels are linked to heart disease. Play also releases endorphins, which help control and eliminate depression. Play lowers the risk of developing a neurodegenerative disease, such as dementia, by increasing cognitive health (Magnuson and Barnett 2013). I think it is safe to say that an hour of play a day keeps the doctor away.

Another benefit of adult play is that it lifts our spirits. It makes us more resilient to stress and helps us stay strong during difficult challenges. Play develops a spiral of positivity that recharges our energy.

Playfulness is part of you, your life, and your world. The more often you play, the more present you are in your playfulness. And the more present you are, the more that playfulness becomes a part of you. When adults are playful, their reward is the pure enjoyment of being fully engaged. Stress is easier to manage, and the focus for educators can shift to more effective and productive practices for working with young children.

Rename and reclaim your stress with this simple exploration.

1. Begin by recognizing the stress.

2. Identify its source. Spend the day tracking your peak times of stress and their causes.

3. Give the stress a name, write it down, share it with a colleague, or yell the name into the air. Better yet, use different media to represent stress in a work of art. The purpose is to release the stress.

4. Rename the stress into something manageable.

5. Identify ways to combat its sources.

Recently I have been feeling incredibly stressed by the extra work that teaching online requires. I noticed that having classes back-to-back is too overwhelming and exhausting. I named this stressor "Nore," for "No More." I wrote it down, shared it with a friend, made a collage in my journal, and on days when the stress was too much, I yelled it into the air. Eventually I changed the name to "Stretchy" to remind myself to get up and stretch in between class sessions. This simple process helped me find an alternative playful action for managing stress. I now take fifteen minutes to stretch, dance, or move in between meetings or classes, which increases my dopamine and helps me refocus.

Ask yourself: How will I play every day to reduce stress? What strategies will I create to help myself incorporate more play into my life?

Play and Playfulness Improve Brain Function

When we play, the brain generates a signal that keeps us coming for more. This is translated into the brain as dopamine, a neurotransmitter that plays a role in how we feel pleasure. Dopamine also affects our ability to plan and think, as it helps us strive to learn, focus our attention, and find passion and interest in life. Play also increases the release of norepinephrine, which triggers adrenaline. Norepinephrine brings us to focused attention and action. When this chemical is present in elevated amounts, it facilitates learning and improves brain plasticity. So not only does playfulness reduce stress, but it also helps increase brain function. Play promotes social interactions, which in turn increase the neuronal networks (Pellis, Pellis, and Broccard-Bell 2010).

As adults, we spend more time accessing our executive functions at the expense of activating the more creative side of our brain. Play allows us to transform. When we play, we can be spontaneous and challenges are easier to tackle. We experience a sense of power and control over our decisions. Play leads us to psychological flexibility and helps us connect to our empathy and create a collective generosity where we support one another.

Play and Playfulness Form an Integral Part of Early Childhood Education

In early childhood education, we value the power of play to support children's learning and development, yet my experiences and observations have uncovered a completely different attitude regarding adults' play. Few programs incorporate playful interactions in their daily work or meetings. Most educator spaces or lounges are not designed for people to take a relaxation break or engage in playful relationships. Instead, they incorporate "keep working" messages. For example, the spaces are equipped with laminators, computers, and photocopiers with a table in the middle for educators to eat lunch and take a break. With space often limited, few early childhood education ecosystems feature outdoor spaces where adults can take a walk. I have seen educators eat in their cars to get away and listen to some music. How do we expect educators to value play and creativity when they are working in spaces that don't value these traits? I propose that when a program creates a culture of play and creativity, it helps educators respect the value of play in their work with children.

Even though we played when we were children, we lack the experience of contemporary childhood (Hendricks 2011). When we fail to recognize this difference, we can fail to see the nuances of current play experiences and representations. For instance, those in my generation spent much of our time playing outdoors, perhaps unsupervised. Technology was not readily available, and we created games to entertain ourselves. Children today spend more time using technology, having been born into a time when screens and digital devices are deeply integrated into the fabric of daily life (Erikson Institute 2016). Perhaps one of the biggest shifts in play that I have observed in the twenty-first century is children's focus on objects (toys) instead of the *action* of play. Likewise, I see how children today are used to what adults consider safer outdoor playgrounds, although these spaces create circumstances where children have a more difficult time learning to navigate risky environments. The good news is that since the 2010s there has been a shift in perspective with the emergence of adventure playgrounds.

Perhaps educational systems don't encourage adult play because it feels like we are losing control. After all, we can't manage or control play. We have to remind ourselves that integrating play and having fun at work is not only related to *what we do* but to *who we are* when we do our job. Having fun is not a reward. It is a process that keeps us creative and enjoying work. When we are filled with wonder and anticipation, we stay motivated to work and bring joy into the classroom ecosystems to benefit children.

I hope you are ready to start rekindling your playful spirit and having fun!

Reflections

- As you read about the research on adult play, what connections do you make to your own playful attitude? In what ways do you see yourself nurturing a playful attitude?

- What types of play influence your work and life? What strategies will you use to bring play into your life?

- How can you bring the element of surprise into your life?

CHAPTER 3

Discover Your Childhood Genius

The small boy [Jung as a child] is still around
and possesses a creative life which I lack. But
how can I make my way to it?

—Carl Jung

When I present to educators, I always include time to play or opportunities for participants to explore their creativity. I am fascinated and sometimes confused by the adults' reactions. Often the first thing I hear is, "You want me to do what?" "Do you want me to play as a child?" or "I don't play." It is apparent that many of us have forgotten how. But adult playfulness is a personality trait and an attitude. It allows us to reframe challenges as opportunities for growth and change. Playful adults look at difficult situations with intellectual curiosity and find them entertaining, engaging, interesting, or a mystery to solve. Evidence of playful adults can be seen in the work of many architects and designers. Ray and Charles Eames played to spark their creativity. Frank Lloyd Wright used Froebel blocks to play and design buildings. Their "childhood genius" was evident in their many creative works.

This chapter explores how rediscovering your childhood genius can help you create playful opportunities to reframe everyday situations in order to experience them as entertaining, intellectually stimulating, and engaging. The chapter also extrapolates ways in which you can interact playfully with others, even during difficult situations. It will help you embrace the conditions necessary to design ecosystems that are playful and filled with joy, and you will learn how to create spaces that support educators in resolving tensions and finding joy in complexity rather than embracing simplicity. The chapter will engage you in valuing unusual activities, ideas, explorations, and objects such as Loose Parts that you can play with freely.

Humans—even adults!—have a long list of universal playful activities we engage in daily: sports, music, art, humor, games, hospitality, dress-up, and flirting. What sets humans apart from other mammals is that we play with words, objects, and symbols. We can also go beyond the literal to create abstract explorations of play—we engage our imagination. Adult playfulness contributes to other life domains, such as intellectual and cultural pursuits, personal involvement, and commitment to social causes. In my case, when I wake up, I spend time sitting outside (weather permitting) and I play a word game on my phone. Or I listen to music and dance. I do something different every day so that I don't get stuck in a routine, and I keep the element of surprise alive. I schedule daily time just to play with Loose Parts or meet with a friend. In other words, I find ways every day to engage in joy.

When we step outside routines and rules, we can fully embrace all the facets of playfulness. We become gregarious, cheerful, and outgoing. We are more expressive and spontaneous, and we may be more willing to try new things. During play, we are more inclined to embrace humor. We also become more dynamic (Proyer 2017). Knowing these facts, we can start to design a playful culture in any organization. Stepping outside the mundane daily rules and routines is necessary to embrace a playful attitude.

Connecting with Our Childhood Genius

Have you ever had a child run up to you in excitement and tell you, "I am the bestest"? Children have the exuberance to embrace their "bestest," until one day when an adult tells them not to be cocky and they stop feeling their "bestest." We mean well—we do want to build their self-esteem, but we also want to define what self-esteem means *for them* instead of letting them define it for themselves. We load them with stickers, praise, and rewards instead of unconditionally accepting their "bestest." In many ways, as adults, many of us have disconnected from our childhood genius, and we no longer have a clear definition of what self-esteem means. In addition to exuberant self-esteem, the genius of childhood encompasses the capacity to love, be flexible, wonder, invent, create, imagine, be profoundly curious, explore, think, dance, and play (Montagu 1989). It is time for adults to explore our childhood genius so that we can connect with our "bestest" and thus support every child's individual, whole best.

When I attended film school, I was fortunate to have the legendary Lucille Ball teach a semester-long class on television production. On the first night of class, she distributed small notebooks and told us to write on the first page, "What will you do for [your name] today?" She encouraged us to tape that message on a mirror and ask ourselves the question every morning. She explained that using our names and answering the question in writing in a journal or notebook helps us create a vision of ourselves as creative, capable, and competent. I remember thinking at the time that she was crazy. After all, I was there to learn about TV production, not engage in self-help. Today I see the wisdom. When we unapologetically give ourselves the gift of reconnecting with who we are, we reembrace our childhood genius.

When you see children playing, you notice they are constantly learning how to do things differently. They work on new ideas and integrate novel solutions to solve problems. They negotiate rules and find ways to let go of old ideas and invite new possibilities. My wise college professor Betty Brady once told me, "Don't tell me something works just because it works. Instead, tell me if something can be done differently to enhance what you are already doing." This quote keeps me continually rethinking and redesigning my internal brain maps. When we play, we are also entering a space where we can question our thinking and redefine our thoughts and ideas. We invite others to argue, discuss, explore, and play with possibilities. This helps us unlearn and relearn while changing the way we make decisions and grow as human beings. We must unlearn habits, perceptions, and myths before we can open ourselves to new thinking, ideas, and knowledge.

● JUST PLAY! CHALLENGE ●

One of my favorite things is exploring different art media to make jewelry. Mixing metals and combining them to find unexpected discoveries as they fuse together is exhilarating. When I give myself the freedom to play and explore, I can embrace my creativity. To create with metals, I had to let go of measuring specific shapes and instead allow the properties of the metal to guide the process. To make jewelry, I learned to celebrate the unexpected discoveries that emerged. Embracing the unexpected is liberating.

Begin meetings with a reconstruction exploration. Invite people to build a tall tower and then carefully take it apart. Ask them to notice what kept the tower standing and how the selection of blocks strengthened the structure. Invite them to share what they discovered and how the insight will help them build a stronger, taller block structure next time. They can then take a challenge they are experiencing in the ecosystem and reconstruct it using the same strategies.

Ask yourself: How will I embrace the unexpected moments and open myself to new discoveries?

Be Flexible

Children constantly challenge adults to adapt to change. We are pushed to unlearn old habits and replace them with new ones, to let go of opinions and assumptions that limit the way we see new ideas and perspectives. More than ever, we have to be flexible to adapt to a constantly moving reality. Being flexible can be very difficult; we commit to our lesson plans and want to be consistent and respected for our reliability. Uncertainty bothers many of us. Sometimes we're too rigid as we transition between explorations. This lack of flexibility can affect the children we care for and educate. Too often I hear educators say, "Since it is not in the lesson plan, I can't introduce it to children." In that instant, the lesson plan becomes more important than the children.

We plan for our future and visualize ourselves achieving our vision of success. In many ways, this commitment to goals is beneficial. It helps us stay productive amid distractions. However, the target moves as other factors change. Perhaps those goals now require more work than expected or that we are willing to do. Maybe we fear we will lose something important, or we now want something else more than we want the original goals. For example, I had a goal of building a successful career in the entertainment industry. My life changed when I became a mother and I realized that it would be too hard to raise a family while working in the industry. Change scared me, and I feared I would have no financial security. Luckily, I opened myself to leave my executive job to become an early childhood educator. I never looked back! Not only am I following my passion now, but my creativity and flexibility have kept me financially stable.

Many of us fear the unknown that comes with change. Not knowing what will happen can prevent us from moving forward and perhaps finding a better reality. When my daughter was three years old, she refused to go down the stairs in our house alone. She believed a monster was living under the stairs and she needed an adult to protect her. We talked about it, and we told her that there was no monster. We looked under the stairs at different hours during the day, but she kept saying that there was a monster. Sometimes trying to convince adults that a certain change will benefit them looks a lot like me trying to convince my daughter that there's no monster under the stairs. The fear of the unknown can be paralyzing. We can't always know whether a change will result in a gain or loss, which can prevent us from taking the risk. I hope that eventually most of us realize that cultivating a willingness to respond to change flexibly can open great creative possibilities that will help us grow.

How often do we use the phrases "This is how we do things around here" or "We have been doing it the same way for a long time, and we do not want to change"? We hold on to outdated traditions or old ways of doing things. It perplexes me how often people do something just because it was done before. They follow the rules without researching or questioning them.

When asked how a particular tradition or practice originated, people seldom give a clear answer. In early childhood education settings, they often say that it is because of licensing or insurance requirements, but when asked when they last reviewed the licensing documents, they just shrug.

When we are open to seeing things from different angles, we can find creative ways to adjust to change. It's never too late to develop your playful, funny, and joyful side. Let go of being self-conscious and give way to your childhood genius. As a child you were naturally playful; you didn't worry about other people's reactions. You can reclaim your childlike qualities by setting aside regular, quality playtime. The more you play, joke, and laugh, the easier it becomes.

Clear your schedule and disconnect every day. Permit yourself to do what brings you joy and engages your playfulness. Be spontaneous, try something new, and enjoy the change of pace. The more we play, the more we let go of meeting expectations.

● JUST PLAY! CHALLENGE ●

Start each day by doing something new:

● Play and dance to new music.

● Drink tea instead of coffee.

● Make an exciting breakfast dish.

● Start a new exercise routine.

What is important is that you do something that challenges you and helps you unlearn old habits. Remember that change takes time, so keep on doing new things. I recently went snowshoeing. It was not my favorite thing to do, but it pushed me out of my comfort zone. I had to unlearn how I walked to incorporate the traction the snowshoes created in the snow. I also had to figure out different ways of getting up when I fell. I found muscles I didn't know I had! I learned that I have to work on my flexibility and strength. Something positive always comes when you play!

Embrace Disruptive Disequilibrium

When I was a child, I liked to pretend to be a trapeze artist, walking on narrow pathways with my arms extended. Sometimes I would pick up a long stick and use it to balance. I'd lay down wood planks and practice walking on them. I climbed on narrow brick walls. When I felt more daring, I would tie a piece of rope about two feet off the ground and attempt to walk across it. I remember the feeling of being unbalanced as I walked on the rope, imagining the fear the real trapeze artist felt as they walked across a thin wire. I tied the rope over a grassy space so that if I fell, I would not be hurt. Having a figurative safety net made me feel better and helped me dare to continue walking. Being in disequilibrium is uncomfortable. However, when we are in disequilibrium, we enter learning. The trick is finding strategies to help get through challenging moments. How do you provoke your own disruptive disequilibrium? When was the last time you metaphorically walked on a rope?

I once worked with an educator who was incredibly resistant to any change. She became highly defensive and controlling whenever she entered into disequilibrium. Her behavior affected the program, including the children. No one wanted to challenge her out of fear of retaliation. Fortunately, the educator finally retired, and then change came quickly.

I learned how important it is to create a culture where disruption is cherished. Instead of always doing the same thing or following a particular practice, embrace your uneasiness and learn to do something differently. Do something you have not done before. Remember that sticking to familiar ways can give you comfort, but it also puts you at risk of losing your place in a world charging rapidly forward. Our ability to maneuver the unfamiliar tests us.

Creating a culture where change is embraced as an opportunity is crucial to strengthening a program and developing strong leaders. Change drives innovation, creativity, and resourcefulness. It's what turns average leaders into visionaries and ordinary programs into extraordinary ones. Educators who can view disequilibrium as an opportunity, rather than a threat, will be leaders in today's educational systems because an ecosystem that leans toward chaos is prime ground for finding creative solutions to setbacks.

Play a game of déjà vu. Think of a challenge or opportunity you're currently facing. Imagine taking a trip into the future to look back to today. How are things different in the future? What will you do to make changes? Perhaps we are stuck in an obsolete paradigm and constricting approaches that limit innovation. We may think that everything has already been invented. However, when we look back through time, we can see that new inventions continually happen. Otherwise, there would be no automobiles, no air travel, no internet, no vaccines, no microwave ovens. How do we prevent ourselves from getting stuck in a noncreative world? We must adapt to change and welcome disequilibrium so that we can create a hopeful future.

Challenge your equilibrium. When I do presentations, I often hear educators' reluctance to let children use real tools. Most of the hesitation comes from fear for the children's safety or fear of being sued or reprimanded.

Setting up different areas for adults to play with real tools (hammers, nails, screwdrivers, drills, and saws) will set educators into disequilibrium. The more we explore tools and Loose Parts that challenge us, the more we will feel comfortable introducing them to children.

Invite educators to explore every tool in detail and suspend their fears and questions. Before play begins, remind them:

1. They can stop if they feel they have entered into territory where they should not be. However, when we are in the habit of backing off, we do not move forward.

2. They can fight their feelings of being unbalanced. However, when we fight and resist, we expend energy in unproductive ways.

3. They can relax, accept, breathe, and talk to you about their feelings. Often when we can accept and explore our disequilibrium as a new way of learning, we move forward in the most profound ways.

After they play, guide a conversation about how to take care of the hazards of using real tools to allow benefits that come with this risky play.

Ask yourself: How did I feel while I was working with real tools?

Be Humble

Have you ever met someone who is too full of their own smartness? They think they have all the correct answers and are fast to respond to questions with the utmost confidence. At times some of us have been that person! Having all the right answers is not a predictor of success. Instead, the best solutions can be found when we are brave enough to admit we *don't* have all the answers or knowledge to solve every problem.

When we embrace humility, we are more open to new ideas, being creative, and listening to one another. Being humble enough to listen to other perspectives can broaden our own thinking.

When we think that we are the most intelligent person in the room, we walk with blinders on but remain unaware of our blind spots. Our minds are closed to new ideas, and our creativity is shuttered. We judge everything as right or wrong, and we want everyone to follow the rules. Thinking that our ideas are the only ideas that exist can result in educators judging children for their willingness to conform and follow the rules—or their lack thereof. This bias leaves the creative children behind until they are ready to serve and follow the rules that have been imposed on them.

When we take the stance of an expert, we end up rejecting ideas and innovation, perhaps because it challenges our ego and questions our expertise. To work past this, we must reflect on our perception of the characteristics of a creative person. A 1999 study found that educators claim to enjoy creativity in children. However, they personally may not want to see some of the characteristics of a creative person, such as nonconformity and messiness (Dawson et al. 1999). I recently had a conversation with a friend who works in education. I mentioned that we could not continue to do the same things in the same way if we want to see a difference in the way we educate children. Their response was an eye-opener to me, a flat-out rejection of anything innovative. They stated that educators could only go so far in bringing innovation and creativity. This comment was the beginning of my interest in reconnecting with our creative side. The answer may not be as complicated as we think. Play promotes creativity, so the more we give adults opportunities to play, the more they will explore their creative spirit and value the traits that define creative children.

Explore humility. Break educators into teams of four or five people. Set a timer for five minutes. Each team writes down as many famous humble people as possible (for example, Gandhi, Abraham Lincoln, Mother Teresa, and so forth). After sharing the lists, explore qualities that define humbleness and explain how the people they named portray these qualities (this may be done in the large group or in breakout groups, depending on the number of participants). After the experience, post a different quality of humbleness each day. Write the word on easel paper and invite educators to draw or write what the word means to them and how they see the word inspiring their practices. Keep all the posts to share at the next meeting.

Ask yourself: What commonalities did I find in the people who display humility in life?

Suspend Time

When I was in third grade in Guadalajara, Mexico, I struggled with math and some other subjects. Unfortunately, the educators had a damaging approach to motivating children. They supplied a math problem for the children to solve individually, and we had to come up to the chalkboard to write the answer once we solved it. The first children to write the correct answer on the chalkboard were called rabbits (fast and capable), the second group called turtles (slow but steady), and the last group was called snails (moving too slow to get anywhere). I never made it past the snail group. This damaged my self-esteem to the point of making me physically ill. I hated school and despised math. The time pressure doubled my anxiety and prevented me from feeling successful. I just could not get in the problem-solving flow. As an adult, I realized that what I really needed was the gift of time. I require time to explore mathematical concepts in different ways. Perhaps these experiences have also affected my own perception of time, to the point of needing to plan every minute of the day to feel productive. The pressure of time adds to the high level of stress in young children.

Children have an easier time suspending time than adults do—until an adult intervenes and limits how long they can play or dictates how fast they need to move. Children can let go and stay in the flow when they are exploring a particular item or idea. As adults, we must find moments when we can suspend the constant scheduling so that we can just go with the flow. We must ask ourselves how we can shift our perception of time to allow ourselves and the children in our care to play without the pressure of meeting outcomes. We must preserve our childhood genius, learn to be fully present, and enjoy every moment. We can begin by understanding that we need the time to experience each moment fully. I recall times I have attended drumming sessions. The sound and the way each drummer comes into the same rhythm helps me get lost in the moment. Another experience that has captivated my intense focus is dancing flamenco. Flamenco dancing requires you to understand the compass (or rhythm), which calls for alternate steps in combinations that give you a twelve-beat musical pattern. Dancing flamenco requires complete concentration, as the rhythm dictates the number of steps you take. Flamenco also uses clapping and castanets, which add to the hypnotic combinations that move through your core.

I recently found my castanets and have been practicing the basics I learned as a child. The repetitive rhythms and nonpitch sounds are very calming. Practicing playing them actually activates my brain and increases my energy.

● JUST PLAY! CHALLENGE ●

Put on some music, and just let your body move to the beat. Explore different rhythms each day. Starting your mornings with play will make a huge difference in how you approach the rest of the day.

Start each meeting with a clapping or drumming session to center people in the moment. This can help them stay present without the constraint of time. Encourage dancing and movement. Dancing to different rhythms or moving to a musical beat can engage our freedom and shift our perception of what is truly important in our daily work.

Ask yourself: How does my perspective change when I engage in a music or rhythm activity? How does it feel when I give myself and others the gift of time?

Be Curious

How often do we adults seek permission or apologize for asking a question? We discourage curiosity instead of inviting people to pursue what comes naturally from birth. Remember the childhood message "Curiosity killed the cat"? Even a well-intentioned quote like that can prevent us from engaging. Being curious must be nurtured into adulthood. Educators must be given the opportunity to play, be playful, and use their creative spirit.

We know that curiosity guides learning, and asking questions increases knowledge. In today's world, learning is not a closed-end enterprise. Learning must be motivated by joy and our innate need to know. The questions we ask can expand or cap our learning. Adults need to engage in curiosity and ask questions to in turn allow children to ask questions. Recently a neighbor was showing a group of us a small chain saw. I was incredibly curious about its uses; I had been looking for a small chain saw that I could easily manipulate. A person in the group responded to my questions in a cynical way: "You use it to file your nails." In that moment, my curiosity was curtailed, and I became silent. When adults instead interpret questioning as an affront to their own capacities, they respond to children in ways that limit their creativity. Therefore it is important to be curious and accepting of others' curiosity, both adults' and children's. This is how we regain our childhood genius.

When we play, we constantly ask questions, explore alternative answers to complex questions, and even consider ideas we never previously thought about. A simple, playful yet transforming exercise is to start a question board. Some simple questions can get you started:

- What are you curious about today? Why?

- What is it?

- What's it for?

- How does it work?

- How do we know that this is the best approach?

- What would happen if I did something different?

- What would this idea look like if I implemented it?

- What are some of the challenges in implementing this idea?

Remember, we are all wired with confirmation bias. Creative responses require us to let go of preconceived notions and humble ourselves. Remember, we do not need to have an answer for everything. Instead, embracing the creative questions here may lead to more questions, and that in turn can change our practices and perspectives.

● JUST PLAY! CHALLENGE ●

Start a collective questions board at work. Use butcher paper or newsprint and sticky notes. Begin by inviting staff, families, and educators to ask questions or wonder about learning. The questions stay up for a week, or longer as needed. Start with silly or fortuitous questions to practice asking. For example, when was the last time you had a lucky streak and everything worked exactly as you expected? If you won the lottery, what would you do? If animals could talk, which would be the rudest?

Once educators are more experienced with asking questions, you can switch to questions more related to work situations. Remember that the purpose is not to come up with answers but to explore the possibilities the questions bring to light, to play with words. Using magnetic poetry tiles or scrapbook letter tiles can add an extra layer of fun to the question board. Once the question board is complete, use it at meetings to analyze the questions and find common threads that may lead to answers. This approach helps me when I feel stuck.

Ask yourself: What am I curious about? What do I want to know about myself and others?

Imagine Opportunities and Possibilities

In his book *Playful Intelligence*, author Anthony DeBenedet defines imagination in adults as an interest in activities and an ability to do things for the pure pleasure of having fun. When we use our imaginations as adults, we are connecting to that childhood genius that allows us to dream and be hopeful. Activities such as reading fiction, painting, and playing imaginative games can strengthen our imaginations and help us use them to solve problems. He states, "At first glance, the link between imagination and psychological reframing isn't obvious. This is because we don't usually think about imagination as a problem-solving tool" (DeBenedet 2018, 21).

Children have tremendous imaginations, and adults can reclaim their childhood genius by embracing their own imaginations. Imagine reading a fiction book that transports you on an adventure or through time. Becoming the main character allows you to explore new parts of yourself. One of my favorite books is *Interview with the Vampire* by Anne Rice. In the book, we meet the vampire Lestat. As I read the book, I can imagine what it feels like to have greater-than-human abilities to manipulate the world. I can also feel Lestat's pain as he reconciles his vampirical desires with his old humanity. His adventures become mine, and my imagination expands.

Imagination closely relates to the idea of daydreaming, or the stream of consciousness that allows us to detach from menial daily tasks. Children have an easier time daydreaming than adults. In daydreaming we find solutions to challenges, create a world where we live in peace with one another, or see ourselves as superheroes. Daydreaming is thinking for pleasure. According to research conducted by a team of psychologists, thinking purely for pleasure is not a common activity, as there is typically a specific activity or purpose tied to thinking. They recommend priming the brain for daydreaming by providing enjoyable and meaningful examples (Westgate et al. 2021).

● JUST PLAY! CHALLENGE ●

Use simple prompts for daydreaming:

● Think of a specific memory from your childhood that brings you joy—perhaps a day that you spent playing with friends or a time you spent outdoors doing something pleasurable.

● Think of something in the future that you are looking forward to—a special social occasion, date, meeting, vacation, or time with friends. Visualize what it will look like, what you will do, and who will be there with you.

After daydreaming, write down your answers or represent them in a work of art. Focus on the emotions. You can also make a collage with photographs that represent both the memory and what you dream for the future.

Ask yourself: How did it feel to represent my daydreams?

Daydreaming is a powerful tool against boredom, and it can be intrinsically rewarding. Thinking is one of the most human things we do, and when we daydream, we become aware of our thinking and use our daydreaming to be innovative. Thinking for pleasure allows us to consider new realities. Just playing and daydreaming is the best form of mindfulness.

Another way to use imagination to solve challenges is to view a scenario as an adventure. Bring this idea to a group, and generate even more possible solutions with collective imagination. Adding humor and looking at the pros and cons of every scenario can keep frustration and negativity away.

When I coach early childhood educators, one of the most difficult tasks is helping people move away from the "they don't let us" mindset. When educators are stuck in that, they have a hard time finding creative solutions. To break away from the "they don't let us" stage, I ask them to imagine what their ideal world or moment looks like. Art can encourage participants to represent their ideal world in a variety of ways. I invite them to work individually or in groups. At the end of the session, they share their dream moments or dream worlds as represented in their art. Then we can begin to talk about various possibilities for making their dreams a reality.

We know that being imaginative is crucial to harnessing creativity and innovation. Many of the advances in technology, consumer products, and science began with the capacity to imagine what the future would be like if things were different. Imagination requires us to let go of existing constructs and see alternate possibilities. We stop clinging to false myths about creativity and find elegant solutions to complex problems because we find hope in what we dream of for a positive future.

Cultivating your imagination as an adult takes practice. When we seek new things, we keep our brains adjusting to challenges. What happens in our brains when we are imagining something? Let's do a simple exercise to demonstrate how imagination works: Put down the book, close your eyes, and envision your favorite food. What does it look like? What are the textures you notice? How does it smell? How does it taste? You probably can create a fairly accurate vision by simply remembering the food and can also recall memories of the person who prepared the food or the people you shared it with. This type of imagination is not hard to do. After all, our past perceptions and experiences guide our thoughts.

Now close your eyes and think of a food you have never eaten before. What does it look like? What are the textures you notice? How does it smell? How does it taste? You are probably having a harder time answering these questions because you have no experiences your brain can harness. Because your brain can't rely on existing connections, you are more willing to use your imagination. When you imagine something you have never actually seen in person, you create different possibilities. You are free just to dream and imagine.

One of the most valuable traits in humans is the imagination. It has been responsible for most of the inventions, discoveries, and ideas produced from the beginning of humanity. Imagination makes the difference in creating a quality work of art—or designing a quality early childhood ecosystem. I see the role of educators as creating disequilibrium that engages imagination, creativity, and thinking.

● JUST PLAY! CHALLENGE ●

Imagine that you are someone else by creating a symbolic persona (avatar) for yourself:

● What is the name of your persona? What will your persona do? What does your persona look like?

● Where will your persona live?

● What magic powers will your persona have?

● Who will be part of your persona's life?

● How will your persona interact with others?

Let your ideas flow and your imagination run wild as you write or draw your persona, and do not edit or question your responses. Instead, ask even more questions. You can change your persona as you explore its qualities.

Ask yourself: What did I learn about myself as I created my persona? What does my imaginary world look like, and how will I include it as I design my ecosystem?

Imagine that you have won the lottery. What will you do?

Visit a museum and immerse yourself in an artwork. What do you think the artist was thinking, feeling, imagining, and exploring when they created the work of art?

Create a vision board with colleagues. A vision board displays images and words that represent your collective ideas about who you are or want to be. Each participant can depict what they do in their individual life and connect it to the collective vision for the organization. Creating a vision board helps identify your intentions, maintain focus, and then transform your intentions into reality. Keep the board in a place where people can see it and add to it daily. The more you view and contemplate your board, the more your wishes enter your subconscious and become a reality. When the vision board is created collectively, it increases connections between people as both the individual and collective visions are made visible.

Take a walk and notice the space around you. Allow your mind to wander and create an imagined world to play in. You might be surprised what it turns up—perhaps a fairyland or the gardens in *Alice in Wonderland*.

Be Playful, Find Joy, and Engage Your Sense of Humor

In chapter 1, we considered the definition of *playfulness* as a state of mind. Bringing more playfulness and laughter into our lives is crucial to happiness, productivity, and inventiveness. As we grow up, we learn to conform, and in the process we let go of the qualities that bring happiness into our lives. In other words, we shed our playfulness and positivity and replace them with responsibility and stress. Perhaps it is time to see life as an ongoing process and realize that we should not grow out of playfulness when we mature. Rather, we should keep on developing it as we age. When we hear a person describe their job as play and not just as a metaphor but as an accurate statement of what they consider fun, exciting, interesting, and challenging, we know that they are engaging in their own playfulness. When I observe people with a playful attitude, they often have a great sense of humor. They see life as something positive, and they are willing to see the funny side of things. They find moments to play and wonder. Playfulness requires us to disregard constraints as we interact with materials and people. When we bring a playful attitude to life, we have more positive emotions and deeper feelings of competence.

Getting together with a group of friends and telling jokes is a lot of fun. My father loved receiving jokes via emails from his friends and delightfully shared them with me. I did not always laugh or enjoy the jokes, but I did enjoy his joy and playfulness as he shared them. He had this incredibly dry sense of humor and was always ready to engage people in laughter. He started a group called *El Club del Chiste* (Joke) and gathered people to share jokes and laugh together. There is nothing more joyful than chuckling with friends or having a belly laugh—the kind of laughter that comes from deep in our core. Joyfulness can be found when we are goofy and playful.

Recently one of my most joyful moments happened at a department store. My colleagues and I had been meeting and sharing some food and fun. We had been talking about creating two cartoon characters named DIP (Developmentally Inappropriate Practices) and DAP (Developmentally Appropriate Practices). We went to a store to walk around and let our food settle. As we entered the store, I casually said, "If you find costumes that can represent DIP and DAP, I will wear them and walk around the store." Of course, one of my colleagues found the perfect chipmunk costumes. So I let go of my inhibitions and allowed my joyfulness to emerge as I put on the costume. We walked around doing a DIP and DAP dance. We laughed together, and it helped us get closer.

Many inventions, discoveries, solutions, and artistic creations are the result of humor, joy, and giving ourselves permission to have whimsical moments. When we embrace silliness to fool around with ideas, play with strange possibilities, or turn things upside down, backward, or inside out, we become more creative and passionate. When we stretch the limits of our imaginations and make room for fun, we enter a state of flow in which our creativity grows. We are then able to innovate, question, and change the rules that constrain our creativity. Humor lets us see things from a new perspective. A riddle or a joke can trigger new ideas. Becoming a character in a book can be engaging. When we can share joy with others, we find intimacy and respect. Joyfulness and humor reduce stress and allow us to develop empathy and a deeper understanding of who we are and the people who surround us. We often feel guilty when we embrace humor during difficult times. However, embracing humor and joy with care, kindness, and appropriate timing can make a difference in supporting people through life's challenges.

● JUST PLAY! CHALLENGE ●

- Write a funny story about something you experienced. Share it with your friends and colleagues.

- Read a funny joke and laugh out loud.

- Have a bubble-blowing competition. The biggest or fastest traveling bubble(s) wins.

- Dress as a clown and visit friends in costume.

- Gather with friends and fly a kite.

- Go to a comedy theater (though if you are attending with others, make sure you agree on what type of comedy is acceptable ahead of time).

- Jump in a mud puddle.

- Skip in the rain.

- Have a water fight.

- Go to a karaoke bar or bring a karaoke machine to work.

- Dress up and act as a superhero for a day.

- Dare to wear an unexpected outfit.

- Share a daily riddle.

Invite Wonderment into Your Life

When was the last time you felt in awe of something? Perhaps it happened when you stood in a picturesque landscape, when you watched a fantastic performance, or when you stood in front of an extraordinary work of art. The world is filled with moments of wonder. When you pay attention, you find you are surrounded by unexpected discoveries. Children are naturally wired to wonder—about their surroundings—about an object, or about how to make something work. Yet somehow as adults we have left wonder behind. We are self-conscious about other people seeing us as we stand with our mouths agape and our eyes wide as we marvel at an event or moment. I invite us all to question ourselves and rethink the lens through which we view life. Can we embrace our childhood genius and invite more wonder into our lives?

There is a place in Mexico where I have found myself submerged in complete awe. It is in the town of Mixquiahuala, Hidalgo. Standing at the edge of the canyon in front of the Cerro del Elefante (Elephant Hill) and listening to the water of the Río Tule (the Tule River) rhythmically move as it travels under the gigantic *ahuehuetes* (weeping willows), is magnetic and hypnotizing. This is where I find my peace and rediscover my creative being. Wondering and embracing a space of awe can be liberating. In Mixquiahuala, I just let go and allow the earth to center me in harmony with the environment. I can claim my creativity and give free rein to my wondering.

Children see the world with awe. They are curious about the smallest details. They look for extraordinary and surprising moments. To see like a child requires us to be open to the possibility that every experience will lead us to a new place we can explore. I love giving children cameras and asking them to take photos throughout the day. Seeing their point of view is exciting. Will I be able to see the world differently? Will the children allow me to discover things I missed?

When I visit a new place, I always wonder, "What would it be like living here? What would I be doing, and who would be surrounding me?" I imagine myself in restaurants and cafés, and I imagine what it would be like to experience art, museums, and daily life. When I wonder, I get a closer connection to the place and notice details that I would not otherwise see.

When you are in awe of something, take the time to wonder and use "wonder-ings," statements that begin with "I wonder." When you see children exploring and creating, use wonderings. Remember that wonderings are not questions for the sake of questions but instead authentic opportunities to foster imagi-nation and curiosity. Wondering together allows us to walk in their space and see things from their point of view.

Go on a walk and look for the little things that spark your curiosity. Take photos and start a collection as a reminder of the wonderful moment.

Celebrate Mistakes

Making mistakes has always been difficult for me. I constantly think about what happened, what I did wrong, and what I need to change. The judg-mental feeling troubles my core, and I don't give up until everything is ana-lyzed. When I took a metalsmith class, I was baffled by the measuring and precision required. I kept failing, and the joy slowly faded away. I am so glad that I did not give up. Every mistake I made led me to discover what I could do and helped me embrace my own style. Eventually I focused my energy on making abstract forms that did not require precision. What emerged was an entirely new perspective and style that I could call mine. I learned that there is profound beauty in abstraction.

The good news for everyone who has a hard time making mistakes is that play and playfulness help us see mistakes as opportunities for creativ-ity and innovation. This is a natural process for children. As adults, we become more sensitive to criticism when we make a mistake. In design thinking, a human-centered process for problem solving that provokes us to solve problems holistically, the term "fail forward and fail fast" is used to describe how failing often leads to the emergence of diverse perspectives that can propel new ideas. Creating space to make lots of mistakes makes us more accepting and appreciative of our own talents and perspectives. Making mistakes allows us to see people, including children, with more respect and compassion. Failing fast fosters the free flow of ideas, shifting mindsets, breaking boundaries, and promoting innovation and sustainable change. When we make mistakes, we learn to be more tolerant of uncertainty, and we are more willing to take

risks and think outside the box (or as I prefer to say, "thinking without a box"). Making mistakes unleashes our full potential and liberates us to do new things by not being afraid to fail and be criticized. Play and playfulness serve as catalysts. They push us to dare to embrace change.

JUST PLAY! CHALLENGE

Make a mistake tree. Cut card stock into leaf shapes. Post the prompt, "What mistake have you made today?" Invite people to write the mistake on a leaf and glue it to the tree. As a variation, people can add leaves of a different color, indicating something they learned or a skill they acquired because they made a mistake. When the tree is full, invite people to celebrate the mistakes and reflect on everything they learned.

JUST PLAY! CHALLENGE

- Push the boundaries of your own risk tolerance by testing something new. Eat a food you have not eaten before. Go on a hike in a new terrain or engage in a sport you have never tried before.

- Tinker with tools. Experiment freely by using tools in different ways. For example, paint with things other than brushes. You can even create new tools to solve specific problems.

- Change something in the ecosystem and test it out. Reflect on what worked well and what needs improvement.

- Play a game you have never played before.

- Mess about, mess about, and mess about again. Try fingerpainting or experimenting with a new recipe. The more you mess about, the more you learn to embrace mistakes as opportunities. I love to mess about in my jewelry studio. I often experiment with new materials. I don't read the instructions; I just mess about. I make a lot of mistakes, but I also discover new techniques that make my work beautiful and intriguing.

Reflections

- How will you create wonderment in your life?

- What strategies will you use to incorporate more daydreaming into your daily life?

- What did you discover about yourself as you explored some of the Just Play! Challenges?

CHAPTER 4

Explore Your Playfulness

If people did not sometimes do silly things,
nothing intelligent would ever get done.

—Ludwig Wittgenstein

In the previous chapters, we defined terms and reviewed the benefits of play. In this chapter, we explore individual approaches to play. Some of us find joy as we explore art or marvel at the power of quietness when we go fishing. Others enjoy being with people and sharing a dance or telling jokes. The adult who exhibited dynamic behaviors in childhood may be happiest when engaging in sports or rough-and-tumble play.

When adults are playful and joyful, we can then bring that joy to children. To create systemic change, we must modify the discourse and carefully analyze our practices. As a professor, when I prepare to start each new semester, I participate in the convocation. I listen to the encouraging messages we always hear from administrators, the typical "Thank you for your service" and "Together we are better." Ideas and programs come and go, and seldom do things really change. We talk, get information, and then are shown how to complete paperwork and meet requirements. I don't know about you, but I feel my energy zapped as I attend these types of meetings. Perhaps it's because we seldom focus on rekindling joy and playfulness.

In spring 2022, I spent two hours at one of these convocations hearing a speaker share her perspective on trauma-informed practices. She let us know how we might be feeling and behaving due to the trauma we have experienced. She suggested that we acknowledge our emotions and share them with others to normalize them. Yes, we have had two challenging years facing the COVID-19 pandemic, but we must also recognize that we overcame adversity and emerged with deep knowledge and respect for ourselves and others. Yes, we are witnessing anger and despair, and we are exhausted. But it concerns me that we pathologize trauma instead of finding positive solutions to generate sustained joy.

Throughout the presentation, I kept wishing that after acknowledging COVID-19's challenges, the organizers had invited a comedian to make us laugh or a magician to inspire our sense of awe or provided games for us to play that captured our interest while bringing us closer together. What we need is laughter, wonder, and fun. We need activities that give us some relief from the ongoing stress. Perhaps if we played more, we would be able to address the trauma triumphantly. Don't get me wrong; I know that many people are experiencing trauma. However, we can't just acknowledge the trauma and believe that will make it go away. Instead, we need to build resilience through play so that we do not promote more trauma in young children.

Regardless of how we engage in playfulness, finding joy is essential to our individual and collective happiness. To create a culture that brings playfulness and joy into our lives and work, we must begin by recognizing how we develop a playful attitude. When we are playful, we are present, responsive, and attentive. We are fully connected to our creativity and ready to let go of constraints. We are ready to accept the invitation to play.

Understanding Your Playful Personality

Who are you when you are with people you trust? Who are you when you let go of your inhibitions and explore new things? Who are you when you dance at a party? Who are you when you gather to have fun? Who are you when you are in the flow of creativity? Recently I attended a conference with a group of close friends. It made a huge difference in my ability to play and connect with other people. We laughed together and we even dressed in 1920s costumes to visit a speakeasy. It was a liberating experience because we dared to play different roles together and walked through history as if we had been part of it.

As I wrote this book, I wanted to learn about other people's approaches to joy and play. I decided to learn more about how fun-seeking, humorous, and playful adults develop their playful approach to life. I have been interviewing my friends and neighbors about what gives them joy and helps them create a playful attitude. One commonality that emerged is that they engaged in unsupervised play when they were children. They shared memories of playing outdoors and going over to neighbors' homes to invite them to come out and play. They shared stories of getting in trouble because they took risks trying something new or following their instincts. Having the freedom to be yourself and make connections with friends gives adults hope and the ability to see the positive side of life. This cheerful and playful attitude was learned in the neighborhood, on the streets, or in the fields where they played.

These conversations elicited the question: How do younger generations who have not had the freedom of unsupervised play develop a playful attitude? When I ask my early childhood college students to look for a play memory, many say that they never played as children. If we have to retrieve childhood memories to connect with our feelings while playing, how can people who never played as children find those emotions? I hope that adults can reconnect with their innate need to play, even if it was stripped in childhood. The answer perhaps is inviting them to play and become part of a playful work culture, to find solace in a space where they can be their authentic, playful selves. They can explore a side of their personalities that has not been engaged for a long time.

Neuroscientist Dr. Stuart Brown has defined eight playful personality types, based on years of observing adults. For the purposes of this book, I have reconfigured and expanded these play personalities and called them archetypes. I share these play archetypes with you with a note of caution. They are not singularly representative of one person. I discourage us from using the play archetypes the same way we have used learning styles to control and enforce our assumptions about play and learning. Instead, I propose that we understand how our personalities are influenced by what we know and what we have experienced in life. Dr. Brown offers a similar warning, "No one is a perfect example of a single play personality type; most of us are a mix of these categories. People might find themselves playing in a different mode than their dominant type at different times and in different situations. I've found that most people recognize themselves in these personalities and find them useful for discovering their own play personality" (Brown and Vaughan 2009, 65). When we are playful, we better engage children in play and create joyful ecosystems where everyone thrives. Embracing our play personality reconnects us with our childhood genius.

The Humorous Archetype

People of the humorous archetype engage in playful nonsense and break into laughter when enjoying simple things in life. Nonsense is at the core of many human engagements from infancy to adulthood. People who enjoy telling jokes or playing harmless pranks engage in the play strategies they learned in childhood. The humorous personality also gets pleasure by making people laugh because they enjoy helping people find joy. I would say my father was an example of a humorous personality. He used his dry sense of humor to make people laugh, and he enjoyed silly toys and gadgets. Children who are boisterous and funny are often criticized and labeled as troublemakers, but this is how the humorous personality plays and makes sense of what is happening.

The Corporal Archetype

People who typify the corporal archetype are constantly moving. They must engage their bodies as they think. My youngest daughter enjoys dancing, walking, and moving her body. She takes hikes and walk breaks throughout the day. The corporal personality can be a dancer, an athlete, a yoga practitioner, or someone who enjoys working out and testing their body's capabilities. They engage in games and activities for enjoyment, not as competition. Children need to move their bodies to understand their capabilities. When adults value their own need to dance, move, and touch, they can better understand the children who keep moving. My hope is that we can honor the corporal personality and stop asking children to sit still and refrain from touching everything.

The Explorer Archetype

We all learn when we are in exploration mode. Explorer types are excited by unexpected discoveries and are fully involved in finding answers or new questions. They may physically engage by visiting new places, climbing a mountain, or testing a new sport. They can explore new feelings through music, attending a play, flirting, or dancing. They may also find pleasure in intellectual endeavors such as designing, hypothesizing, and testing new ideas and experiments. They may engage in debate from the pure interest of learning new perspectives. Both my daughters are explorers. They look for new adventures and new places to visit. They try out new activities and enjoy engaging in different physical activities. I would say that I am an intellectual explorer. I am in constant search of knowledge and new experiences. Children who move from one exploration or activity to another are often seen as unfocused. I venture to say they are absorbing, feeling, hypothesizing, and giving meaning to their actions.

The Competitor Archetype

Competitors seeks the adrenaline rush of contests, rivalries, and face-offs. They play games with rules, keep score, and strive to win. Competitors look for acceptance in social groups by dominating or being the top person. Competitors also enjoy competing against themselves, whether through games such as solitaire or through striving to best a previous record or achievement. I will use my father again as an example. He was passionate about soccer and spent hours watching it on TV and attending matches. Being an observer was not enough. Instead, he became actively involved in the board of directors of Las Chivas Rayadas, one of the premier soccer teams in Mexico. Children who organize games and seek to win are finding their leadership abilities, learning too that competition requires persistence and empathy. Next time you feel the urge to prevent children from being competitive, stop to observe what they are doing and experiencing. You may be surprised that when children create competition, they are also developing social skills such as negotiation and adaptation.

The Director Archetype

The director enjoys the power of guiding and telling people what to do. On a visit to Children's Circle Nursery School, I witnessed a group of children playing "movie." One child had eagerly assumed the role of director. When the others stopped listening to him, he would yell, "Cut! I said cut." I know many adults who take the role of directors. They tell others what to do and how to do it. The director archetype seeks to prevent chaos by taking control and flourishes when there is a sense of trust and security so that they may lead others to play.

The Collector Archetype

Those who embody the collector archetype collect for pleasure, to learn more about the objects, to seek status or prestige, or to show loyalty to a team, country, or hometown. Anyone who collects Loose Parts exemplifies this playful approach. I know that I seek the thrill of finding that new object and analyzing it for its play affordances. My mother collected state quarters for every grandchild. The joy of finding them kept her looking, and she engaged other family members to help her. Other adults gather items for the pride of having the best, most comprehensive collection of objects or experiences. My nephew enjoys the experience of mixing and drinking a new cocktail every week. He keeps a record of the concoctions he discovers. He researches each new drink carefully and then shares his findings on social media. Like my nephew who collects cocktail recipes, can you identify the children who collect rocks and other knickknacks? They often want to take things from school and bring them home. They are collecting for pleasure.

The Artist/Creator Archetype

Many people find joy in creating art and making meaningful things for themselves and others. They become skilled at crafts such as jewelry making, printmaking, knitting, crocheting, and so on. Sometimes the goal is to make something beautiful or functional. Other times, it is the process of learning and practicing a new skill that provides joy. Many of the artists I know love to play with all types of challenging materials, and the pleasure is in the discoveries they make. I love to play with fire and move metal with a torch. The unexpected discoveries make my heart beat harder, and I can sometimes be seen jumping up and down in my jewelry studio celebrating my creations. When adults value their own creativity and innovation, we become more accepting of children's experimentations. I hope that we stop asking children to re-create adult-designed crafts (what some call "craptivities"!) and instead let them explore the artist-creator archetype.

The Storyteller Archetype

We all have a storyteller within us. Storytellers are performers, writers, and screenwriters. They lose themselves in books, movies, or theater. My neighbor David pointed out that storytelling is at the heart of Jewish humor. Patrick, another neighbor, is an engaging storyteller. He keeps us enthralled and laughing. A commonality among storytellers is imagination. I have a childhood friend who became a magician. As he performs his magic tricks, he becomes different characters and captivates you with storytelling. Choreographers, such as my favorite, Alvin Ailey, can elicit every human emotion in beautifully choreographed dance pieces. Children are born storytellers who share the most amazing stories. Actively listen as they tell stories in dramatic play. My hope is that when we learn to value our stories and share them with others, we will be more open to listening to the stories children tell us.

The Producer Archetype

The producer personality is defined by the need to organize and produce new play adventures, parties, gatherings, and explorations. Producers are engaging and willing to take charge to ensure that an activity is successful. They are full of ideas and do not hesitate to share them widely. I could classify myself as a producer. I love to organize parties and adventures. I love gathering people and creating experiences. The downfall is that I often forget to ask others what they want to do before moving forward with a plan. I sometimes have a hard time going with the flow when things are not planned. Perhaps times like this are when a playful adult can gently serve as a resource to help children maneuver the sticky points of being a producer. Producers often pair with a director to guide the playing.

The Advocate Archetype

Advocate children and adults have tremendous awareness of group dynamics. They speak up when they perceive unfairness and inequity and pursue the restoration of social justice. They look to include everyone and engage empathy and compassion in all aspects of play. The advocate archetype constantly facilitates discussion and mediates arguments that happen in play. My youngest daughter has this innate characteristic. As a child she was always aware of who was included and would argue when she felt that play was not inclusive. Her intentional approach to inclusivity always invited people to see the bigger picture.

The Negotiator Archetype

This archetype comes out when a child or adult argues every step in a process. They know what they want, and they are patient and persistent. They come up with creative approaches to negotiate. They listen and then share their views. They are skillful at reading social cues. I once observed two children arguing about the amount of water needed to fill a pitcher. The negotiation got heated, and an educator approached them and asked, "Do you need help?" The negotiator child responded, "No, I will talk her into it." I continued to observe, and in the end, both children agreed on the quantity of water needed to fill the pitcher. When playful adults recognize that negotiations are a part of play, they can react to children's arguments and conversations with more understanding. After all, everything in life is a negotiation. We negotiate the way we use materials, we negotiate to get our needs met, and we negotiate when we make friends and build relationships.

The Debater Archetype

This archetype is indicated by a willingness to see every point of view, analyze every angle, and find multiple solutions to a single challenge. When I see children discussing a problem, often there is one child who is motivated to test every idea presented. They will argue multiple perspectives and invite other children to listen to one another. They are confident, articulate, and persuasive. My great-nephew Diego is a debater. At an early age, he articulated what he wanted, looked at different perspectives, and then made his own decision. Diego can effectively debate among the best and clearly make his point of view known, sometimes to find consensus and sometimes just to make his thinking known without expecting a specific response. He fights for the rights of people and will continue to discuss his way through life.

Engaging Adults in Play

I want to reiterate that these play archetypes are not meant to classify people into different categories. Instead, they help us understand that we all enter play and playfulness from different perspectives. Remember:

1. You can have multiple play archetypes and do not have to identify as a specific one.

2. Your play archetype can change throughout your lifespan.

3. Various types of playfulness exist in each archetype.

I include these play archetypes to help you plan a playful culture and ensure that we have an ongoing system that values and invites all types of play. The following are some ideas that can guide your practices with that in mind. My hope is that when you combine them with the tenets of play (see chapter 1), you will gain a robust culture of play in your organization.

Perhaps the first place to start creating a playful culture is by asking people to identify a playful archetype that resonates for them. However, it is also important to remind them that they can embrace other playful archetypes as they spend more time playing.

Rough-and-Tumble and Physical Play

Although it may look different from when children do it, adults do engage in rough-and-tumble play. It is an active play exploration—movement, dancing, tug-of-war, capture the flag, scavenger hunts, and more. Physical or body play also includes the desire to liberate ourselves from gravity—yoga, Pilates, meditation, adventure play, zip-lining, trampolines, and aerial gymnastics. And of course there is nothing as enjoyable as swinging on a swing.

Some of my fondest memories of my career emerged from participating in community development and think tanks. I enjoyed these interactions because we not only played with words and ideas but also engaged in adult rough-and-tumble play. One of the most memorable moments happened when two executives from large agencies started wrestling. It was unexpected and brought laughter and fun into a profound moment. They were good friends and had known each other for a long time, so the wrestling was in jest. This moment when they embraced their corporal archetype through rough-and-tumble play gave us the necessary relief we needed to spark creativity. From then on, we purposely planned moments to dance, go on walks, and enjoy physical activity.

We often shy away from rough-and-tumble play because we find it aggressive, yet it is stimulating. For example, using foam or paper swords to fence each other is energizing and engaging. Fencing requires strategy and deep thinking, and it fires endorphins that promote relaxation. Rough-and-tumble play helps us develop emotional regulation and cognitive, emotional, social, and physical mastery. From a group perspective, rough-and-tumble play highlights the importance of playful teasing and supports us in reading body cues. Maintaining a focus on joy and pleasure needs to be the unwritten agreement.

● Take a dance class that invites your body to move. Salsa, flamenco, tap, or any other style can stimulate your body, mind, and creativity. I love the energy of a line dancing group. There is something magnificent about moving in unison.

● Spend an afternoon at a local park swinging with a friend. Take turns pushing one another. Notice how your body feels as you pump the swing to move faster.

● Join a community sports league or invite friends to join you in a friendly game of handball, baseball, or soccer, or something that requires less coordination and organization like Frisbee or bocce ball.

● Take a fencing class—many community centers offer recreational fencing. Invite a group of friends to a mock sword-fighting party, and roll newsprint or butcher paper into long pieces to make paper swords for fencing matches.

● Bring out scarves and ribbons and move freely to your favorite music. I love flamenco, and I enjoy playing the castanets while breaking into some flamenco dancing moves. The energy helps me get the day started.

● Go zip-lining with friends.

Ask yourself: How do I feel as I include more active play in my life?

Habitude Play

Habitude play includes board games and projects with collaboratively negotiated rules and structures. We create, strategize, design, and engage in activities that bring people together for a common goal. Habitude play reengages us with our playfulness and gives us permission to just have fun. When you have fun, you are more fun to play with, which makes the game more fun. When the game is more fun, everyone wins. Habitude play can be engaging for the producer and director archetypes. They enjoy organizing and guiding others into specific forms of play.

When you are fully immersed in a game, your focus is on the players, their strategies, and what will happen next. It's almost as if you are released from the responsibility of what might be happening outside the game and in the realities of life. When you end the game, you emerge reawakened, perhaps more open to the world and what it has to offer.

It is essential to rethink the idea of winning. Games are fun because they let us explore our authentic selves both individually and as members of a team. When we win, we feel bigger and more confident. When we win, we are larger than life. When our team wins, we feel big because we are part of a *we*. When you are part of a *we*, you become part of a larger concept, and your *me* gets stronger, even when your team loses. Think about how the competitor archetype enjoys competitive games. In the words of Bernard De Koven, author of *A Playful Path*, "Playing together, we discover trust. Laughing together, we discover harmony. Through play and laughter, we transcend tragedy, we challenge our physical limits, we celebrate health, we create community, and we redefine the daily game" (De Koven 2014, 162). Losing is not measured as a negative but rather understood as a process of strengthening community. I know that it sounds like a contradiction, but when we see losing as something that just happens, we can regroup and reclaim our joy. We also must remember that it is not about the game but the people who are part of the game. When we gather with a group of people to play games, we become part of a community.

● JUST PLAY! CHALLENGE ●

● Start a game night or weekly game of cards with friends and neighbors. It does not need to be for money; try playing for candy or any other "wins" you agree on.

● Search for local restaurants and venues that host trivia and invite a group of friends to join you for trivia night.

● Gather friends or coworkers to share stories of how you had fun as a child.

● Carry a play object in your purse as a reminder to have fun. I carry a rock I found on my final visit to my children's nursery school.

● Play and choose to have fun daily. Make a list of all the ways you have fun every day.

Ask yourself: What will I carry with me that reminds me to play more every day?

Imaginative Play

Remember when you were a child and you let your imagination run wild until your fantasies became reality? This is what imaginative play is all about! Music, storytelling, painting, drawing, collaborative transient art, creative hobbies, and acting foster our imagination through play. I remember as a child playing out space fantasies with friends in the park. We called a cluster of trees in the park our spaceship. We gathered after school and on weekends and played for hours. Our scripts got more sophisticated with time, and we changed locations in the park to represent our imaginations better. As an adult, I have participated in a few steampunk events and dressed up to go to the yearly Dickens Fair in San Francisco, California. During these events, I transform myself into a Victorian steampunk traveler and join a fantasy world. By transforming, I connect to emotions that had been inhibited for a long time. I let go of my fears of being criticized and suspend my fear of what people think of me. I feel free to be me without restraints, and the freedom is exhilarating as I reconnect to my adventurous self, embrace my explorer archetype, and allow myself to travel in time.

At other times, I daydream and imagine my life to be different. "What would my life be like if . . . ?" Yes, sometimes it is challenging to realize that life could be different, but there is a glimmer of hope when we learn that we have control over our thoughts and the choices we make. Imaginative play allows us to explore the unknown future and imagine a different reality from the current moment. In our imagination we dream and ponder, revisiting our thoughts and ideas. I urge us to constantly imagine and consider our dreams as possibilities for hope and joy.

Imaginative play helps us develop abstract, higher-level thinking as we innovate to solve complex problems. It allows us to create tools, ideas, and artifacts that improve our quality of life. Recent research conducted at the University of Colorado in Boulder has confirmed that our imagination has a way to regulate anxiety (Reddan, Wager, and Schiller 2018). When we imagine an event or an experience, it influences our perception and cognition and can affect our emotions. Imagination induces neural plasticity. It increases flexible thinking and enhances our interactions with the real world.

I love visiting museums and art galleries. I sit in front of a painting or sculpture that invites me to linger and look closely. I try to imagine how the artist felt when they created the work of art. I imagine how the artist explores the different analogies and metaphors that make it into the composition. On one visit to the Museum of Modern Art in New York, I stumbled into Paul Cézanne's exhibit. What fascinated me was how Cézanne played with the concepts of time and contemplation. I have visited the studios of many artists throughout my life, and when I ask what their inspiration is, they often reply that it is an image they have in their head. Every one of us sees life from diverse angles and perspectives, so I would capture the details of an image in one way while another person sees something different. I think that is why I love abstract art. It allows the viewer to interpret the piece without precisely knowing the artist's intent. In a way, the viewer uses imagination to decipher how they feel about the work. The beauty is that our imagination can be as big as we want it to be.

● Play the metaphor game. Notice something in your environment and turn it into a metaphor. For example, I see a dandelion breaking ground during my morning walk. I think about the dandelion as a metaphor for survival and strength. When I see the sun in the morning, I connect the sunshine to the people in my life who make me happy. Thinking in metaphors supports the development of imagination. After all, life is but a metaphor.

● Play with analogies. Analogies in imaginative play are created through the divergent thinking process (the basis of creativity). Select an image from a magazine and describe it by using only analogies. See how many different ideas you can conjure.

● Improvise. Let go of the to-do list and stop planning for one week. Instead, imagine what it would be like just to go with the flow. Engage and be fully present in what is going on around you. Right now, imagine how you would feel if you did not have to plan constantly.

● Go on a nature walk with zero expectations. Pretend that you are a different person—perhaps a character in a book you just read. What would it be like for that character to go on this adventure? What would the character do? What would the character notice?

● Next time you have to wait for something or someone, spend time imagining what else you could be doing. Create a mental adventure in which you are the superhero.

● Look at the sky and read the clouds. What do they remind you of? I also do this with ceiling tiles and floor tiles. I find shapes and imagine what they mean.

● Organize a "who did it" mystery game. Ask people to dress up (or have props available) and take on roles.

● Create an imaginary playground in your mind. Explore it and think about the skills you need to maneuver the space, like exploring a 3-D level in a video game. Is the playground in the treetops? Underwater? In outer space? Do you have new or magical abilities when you enter the playground?

Narrative Play

Narrative play, in its simplest form, helps us see the stories behind our play and the daily playful moments in our lives. This form of play gets people who resonate with the storytelling archetype to fully embrace the moment and thrive. Narrative play helps us look for changes, emerging ideas, and concepts. It can also help us share our collective lives. We can learn from one another's mistakes, perspectives, and ideas.

Creating opportunities for adults to share stories and play with narratives can be a powerful way to convey values and offer insights into one another's perspective and knowledge. It begins by creating a culture where stories are valued and promoted as a risk-free vehicle to build trust and a sense of belonging. Share a story of part of your life and how that moment took you to where you are today. The narrative guides the conversation as your group collectively learns from the experience.

The stories of my childhood are embedded in all the things I do. The feeling of awe and spiked curiosity remains with me. I recall the stories I read in books and the stories the adults in my life have shared: the stories of how my paternal grandparents emigrated from Russia to find a better life, of how my maternal grandparents got through the Depression, and of how my parents met and eloped. All these stories connect me to my family's history.

Storytelling forges connections between people and ideas. When we tell stories, we can laugh together, find commonalities, and create a culture of respect and playfulness. Stories we hold in common are a vital part of the ties that bind us together. Invite educators into narrative play by providing opportunities to reenact their experiences through role play, journal writing, and guided games that include creating and acting as a specific character (such as murder mysteries or "whodunit?" games).

I share my stories in my writing and also reenact them as I create avatars for imaginative and dramatic play. For example, when I attend a steampunk convention or Renaissance faire dressed in costume, I assume the role of a time traveler making meaning of my ancestors' journey from Russia to find their home in Guadalajara, Mexico. Using the lens of my ancestors' experiences allows me to view their pain and challenges and helps me appreciate the gift they gave our family by providing stability and wealth.

Narrative play is a powerful tool when we are learning something new and working to find the logic behind it. For example, when we imagine how things worked in the past, we can create a narrative that leads to change. Our understandings take shape as we construct the narrative. We can confront what we don't know and begin to identify the pieces that are missing or do not fit. As we uncover the story, we make our own learning visible to ourselves and to others. The telling of stories turns us into the actor, as we move from generating an idea to clearly linking it to our own experience. You do not have to become a professional actor to play a role in a collective narrative. Instead, you can create a culture where each story is valued and find ways to unravel the collective consciousness for yourself and others.

JUST PLAY! CHALLENGE

- Create a map of your own story. Get a map and identify each place that brings up a life memory. Mark the identified place on the map with a dot. Allow the story to emerge before you analyze it. Just play with your thoughts and memories.

- Begin the morning by telling a story about how you will play. It can be as simple as playing with an idea or image of what your day will look like. What will you do to be playful? Where will you go to share your playfulness? How will you play?

- Create personal narrative play cards. At the end of each day, take an index card and write a play journey you can engage in the following day. Keep it simple: a walk in the park, playing a game with friends, or dancing to your favorite music. As you experience the play journey (or soon after), write on the back of the card your feelings and emotions to uncover your learning in the moment. Do not throw your cards away; keep them to revisit and reuse.

Retell a classic story by becoming the main character. Imagine who you want to be in the story. Will the role change? Will the story change? How will you rewrite the ending? Daydreaming is a powerful way to imagine new perspectives and play with narratives.

Ask yourself: Where and how can I incorporate more storytelling in my daily interactions?

Object Play

Object play can encompass building and playing with Loose Parts, such as big planks with tree stumps and small tree cookies with blocks. Manipulation of objects, construction, and design fall into this play category as well. Loose Parts support play archetypes because people are in control of the action. The items are just a vehicle to engage creativity and critical thinking. For instance, object play is inviting to collector archetypes, who enjoy finding unexpected discoveries to add to their collections.

In 2012 I was first introduced to Loose Parts play at the Good Stuff for Children conference. Bev Bos, a mentor and friend, had created incredible opportunities for adults to play. She organized a room filled with Loose Parts and invited us to play silently for thirty minutes. She asked us not to have any conversations and to fully focus the body and mind on play. Lovely music was playing in the background. At first I struggled to get into the flow, but eventually my creativity led me, and time flew by. It was an extraordinary feeling to let go for a moment and focus my full attention on being present. We listened to our breathing and the sounds the Loose Parts made as we moved them.

Perhaps tinkering is the ultimate object play. When we tinker, we repair, connect, adjust, and use objects to experiment. Tinkering allows us to explore real phenomena that we can see and touch, gaining a deeper understanding of STEM concepts. Tinkering allows me to test out ideas and find creative ways to express them. I love moving and changing the properties of metal with fire. Tools are a big part of my tinkering in the jewelry studio—hammers with various textures, tweezers, files, saws, a flex shaft (a drill and sander tool), and especially the torch! One of the things that I enjoy the most is finding the right tool to help me solve a problem. The other advantage of my tinkering is that I am not applying direct math, which frightens me. Instead, I have learned to embrace a more abstract, nonlinear approach. You do not need to own many tools and materials to tinker. Nuts and bolts, wires, and items that connect and disconnect can get you started. You just need curiosity.

Object play includes working on puzzles: jigsaw puzzles, puzzle games, and even games such as chess. Puzzles ask us to manipulate objects, balance things, fit things together, and play with others. They engage our intellect and challenge our creativity. Some puzzle games require us to react quickly, while others invite contemplation. Puzzles also allow us to make mistakes and find solutions. I enjoy puzzles because they challenge our abilities and teach us that we can do more than we initially thought. One of my favorite types is moving-piece puzzles, in which the same piece fits in several places.

One of my favorite types of object play involves buttons. Buttons inspire intricate designs of transient or ephemeral art. They also engage us in conversation and storytelling. Each button has a story and perhaps offers the personality of the person who collected the button. A container of buttons engages the senses of touch and hearing as well as sight. Sometimes when I am stressed, I take out a box with buttons and just put my hand in, to feel the textures and hear the sounds the buttons make. It is relaxing and helps me focus.

During my Loose Parts presentations, educators enjoy constructing with cardboard tubes, paper cups, and cardboard ramps. The laughter around the room is invigorating. An incredible sense of joy brings people together. You can hear everyone negotiating and collaborating to test their ideas. There is something extraordinary about watching adults immersed in play.

● JUST PLAY! CHALLENGE ●

- Spend time tinkering. Focus on something you enjoy doing. Do you like connecting pieces? Making robots? Creating ephemeral art?

- Put a puzzle together and then take it apart. I find as much pleasure in deconstructing the puzzle as I do in constructing it.

- Buttons, buttons, buttons! Create a piece of ephemeral art using buttons. Take a photo and keep it in a journal to celebrate your creativity.

- Design and construct with blocks or other Loose Parts.

- Visit an adventure playground with large Loose Parts and spend time playing.

- Create cairns on your hiking adventures and in your garden. I find much pleasure in photographing stone structures created by people.

Design Play

In design play, we use Loose Parts as tools. What is important is not just the object but also the actions we create when we interact with the object and discover how to move forward in our quest for playful change. In writing this book, I came up with the concept of design play as I researched the process of design thinking. When people engage in design thinking and design play, they increase their creative capacities and refocus their energy to find answers to complex challenges.

We often do the same things as we move through the day, day after day. To engage our creativity and generate innovative concepts, we need to diverge from our routines and habitual ways of thinking that may be holding us back. We must allow room to experience new challenges and discover new opportunities. When we play, we enter into a world of divergent thinking. Divergent thinking is a creative, nonlinear, free-flow, out-of-the-box thinking that ignores limitations and constraints to generate multiple possible solutions to a design problem.

Design play builds bridges between colleagues, creating opportunities to connect, listen, and respect the diversity of thoughts and ideas. Adults who identify with the art/creator archetype fully engage in this type of collaborative work. When we build connections with people and materials, we are weaving a platform where innovation emerges. Decisions are no longer in the hand of one person who approves or disapproves but are made as a team. Design play can create a safe space where all input is welcome, no matter one's job title or seniority within an organization. Loose Parts have a powerful and liberating quality that allows us to see diverse perspectives.

Another benefit of design play is that it grounds you in the present moment. Imagine yourself tinkering with a variety of Loose Parts and tools. You have an idea that you want to work out, perhaps changing an aspect of the early childhood ecosystem to make it more accessible. You can use Loose Parts to create a prototype that helps other people visualize what is needed and in the process redefine licensing and quality rating expectations.

Often we face an inner critic who tells us that we are not doing things right. Play helps us shut that off and disconnect the analytical brain to avoid analysis paralysis. In play you let the materials guide you, and you get into the flow. All of a sudden you are generating ideas, not questioning them but just letting them propagate. Each idea triggers your curiosity and keeps your ego away.

Design play helps us see what I call "and" solutions. For some reason, we have been programmed to constantly give "No" or "It can't happen" answers. Fortunately, with design play, we trust that we can discover multiple solutions to our most challenging problems. Perhaps that is why so many ideas come to me when I create polymer clay beads with abstract designs, when I explore different media, or when I design a transient work of art. In the process, I generate solutions that lead to more innovative products. What I know is that when we turn off our inner censors and think expansively, we can produce amazing ideas, promoting the "and" mindset.

● JUST PLAY! CHALLENGE ●

- Create a space where you can tinker with design play. When life presents you with a challenge, it is easy to jump into problem-solving mode. Instead, give yourself time to engage in design play in your space. Your brain will release the fear and stress brought on by the challenge, and you will begin to find more creative solutions.

- Bring a semi-abstract drawing and ask educators to generate a list of possible ideas for what that picture might represent. There is no right or wrong answer, just a list of possibilities.

- Bring a variety of Loose Parts and invite educators to design a tool to solve a problem they are currently facing.

- When a challenge comes to you, begin by playing with the most desirable outcome. Use art materials to explore what the desired outcome could look like. You can also create a collage or take photographs to help visualize what you want. Once you have a clear concept of what outcome you want to see, start visualizing the steps you need to achieve it. This means starting from the end goal and following a path back to the current state of things. Do not skip steps even if you think you have solved that part of the challenge. Remember that the learning is in the design play process.

Celebratory Play

As humans we enjoy celebrating holidays and the special moments of life. What fascinates me is that many of us have a love-hate relationship with celebrations. We want to feel proud of our accomplishments, but that inner critic tells us not to brag. We want to celebrate wholeheartedly, but when we do, we suddenly become aware of what other people may think. Even more concerning is that we seldom celebrate our individual and collective accomplishments.

I propose that we engage in a daily dose of celebratory play to summon our creative spirit, reconnect with our roots, and soar toward a new vision. Celebratory play touches our hearts, fills us with pride, and frees our imaginations. It can be as simple as celebrating a funny moment that happened that day or a bigger team achievement. What is important in any organization is creating a celebratory tone that uses play as the center of daily work.

Children know how to celebrate their wins and their mistakes. As adults, we must learn to do the same. When children play "birthday party," they put their entire selves into organizing the celebratory play. When they build a block structure, they celebrate with a scream of delight—perhaps by knocking it down! Adults must find simple ways to celebrate relationships. We must celebrate a colleague's accomplishments. We must learn to celebrate life, and what a better way to do it than by engaging in play? Fly kites, blow bubbles, play with pinwheels, or dance around a maypole. Better yet, do a different celebratory thing every day. Start by creating a list of objects that mean *celebration,* and celebrate by playing with every item in that list.

When we celebrate alone, we begin to recognize that our accomplishments have meaning and that we should not feel judged or ashamed of celebrating them. We begin to recognize and value our capacities so we can share them with others. Celebratory play can help us rewrite the script in our head so that we no longer feel "cocky" or like a "show off" for accomplishing something great.

When shared with people, celebratory play can reinvigorate our collective work and instill a sense of wonder, meaning, and joy. It can help us build relationships, relieve tension, and create excitement in our lives. When I turned sixty years old, I threw a party to celebrate the idea that "the future is female." I invited all my beautiful women friends to play, drink, and have fun together. There was a photo booth to take pictures, a book to draw messages, art materials to explore, and games to play. My fondest memory is when we went around the circle celebrating one another and our relationships. Hearing what my friends said about me made me feel proud, and articulating how they had influenced my life increased my joy.

Celebratory play must be authentic and not contrived by ongoing awards and praise. It comes from a shared vision and common values. During my career in the entertainment industry, in one of the companies where I worked, the administration integrated celebratory play throughout the culture. Celebrations included ways to give feedback and increase our knowledge of the company's products. Management valued employees' contributions and constantly provided us ways to celebrate new productions collectively. For example, there were raffles to win the opportunity to give feedback on a new show or movie that we were testing before making it public. Raffle winners were invited to a nice lunch to watch the show or movie and even received a personalized gift. At other times we celebrated together by attending the horse races or a play. Fun, laughter, and a playful attitude were encouraged. When we stayed late to complete a project, the company provided dinner and we would play even as we worked. In retrospect, the company had a playful culture because it saw human contributions as its most valuable asset. Your organization doesn't need to have a lot of money to instill celebratory play. It is the mindset that has no price.

We seldom celebrate the mistakes we make, but doing so can be greatly liberating and propel us forward. Let's celebrate mistakes as possibilities for growth and change. Celebratory play helps us embrace mistakes, decrease our fear of failure, and take risks that can lead to innovation. When mistakes are welcome and seen as a learning process, we become free to experiment and grow in our thinking and capacities. Celebrating mistakes as discovery engages our creative capabilities and helps us find more innovative approaches to what we do. By celebrating mistakes, we learn about the strengths and needs of the people with whom we work, building our empathy and helping us walk in someone else's shoes.

- Celebrate mistakes with empathy and care. Take the time to do something that brings you joy when you make a mistake. The joy will help you see that there is light at the end of the tunnel (not a train coming at you!) and that the learning can propel you forward.

- Celebrate the changing of the seasons by spending time outdoors. Fresh air brings renewal to our entire being. Take advantage of beautiful weather when you can, even if that means simply opening a nearby window. Fresh air reminds us that life is worth living.

- Celebrate by playing a game with a group of your friends. Organize an impromptu game of cards or, better yet, an active game of Frisbee. Whatever game you choose, celebratory play brings friends together.

Culture/Identity Play

Every culture has its own varieties of humor and playfulness integrated into its tapestry. I will only address humor that is representative of my cultural background, and I invite you to do the same. Do not attempt to appropriate humor, jokes, or playfulness from cultures that are not your own. Find pleasure in the playful aspects of your culture. Harness the memories that bring you joy.

I grew up in Mexico and was enveloped by Mexican humor and double meanings. I remember a book called *Picardía Mexicana*, which roughly translates to "Mexican Naughtiness." Mexican oral tradition has this adage: "*En cada refrán, una verdad*" ("In each saying, there is a truth"). My Mexican identity is connected to many of these sayings and the culture's sense of humor. It was part of my household and part of my social interactions. In many ways, these expressions permeate my identity and, I think, the identity of many Mexicans. Some of the moral values behind the sayings help me better understand both my family and social expectations. When family and people close to me want to share a moral value, they often use a traditional phrase that clarifies the acceptable societal behavior.

A perspective that emerged in my conversations with friends and neighbors included the place of humor in Jewish households. My neighbor David, who has a fantastic sense of humor, remembers how people often have gathered in his home to share stories. He explained to me that the strong tradition of storytelling and humor in Judaism has supported Jewish survival and the preservation of traditions and values. The folklore, stories, jokes, proverbs, and even curses have been passed along throughout the generations. As David shared during our conversation, Jewish humor is optimistic, joyful, and celebratory. He enjoys making people laugh and will make an effort to change a negative or sad discussion.

Traditions of storytelling, sharing laughter, and humor can help us better understand our individual cultures. Inviting educators to compare and contrast how humor was used in their childhoods can bring them closer together. Sharing with other educators the games we played in childhood can also help people connect. Because they are influenced by local culture and environment, traditional games can teach us about a country's people, language, geography, climate, animals, resources, and more.

● JUST PLAY! CHALLENGE ●

- Reconnect with your childhood and rediscover a game you played growing up.

- Gather with friends and invite them to bring a board game from their culture. Sharing cultural games can teach about the history and traditions that are close to our hearts.

- Explore humor from your culture and share some memories of how humor helped you survive difficult circumstances.

- Think of a game that you enjoy playing with friends and family, and share stories of how the game has brought you together. Notably, games and play are not only an opportunity to practice a mixture of analytical and creative thinking but also a safe place to make mistakes and test new ideas.

Ask yourself: How does bringing games from my childhood help me connect with others? What have I learned about myself? What have I learned about others?

Reflections

- What will you do to engage your playfulness?

- How will you offer more opportunities for humor, laughter, and play at work?

- How do you see your imagination helping you to unlearn and disrupt your current practices?

- What will you do to create spaces where mistakes are celebrated as opportunities for change?

CHAPTER 5

Lead with Play, Lead to Transform

The fact is that given the challenges we face, education does not need to be reformed—it needs to be transformed.

—Sir Ken Robinson

Leadership is often associated with seniority, specific expertise, a title, personal attitudes, or the ability to manage a company or workplace. Leading people to embrace a playful attitude requires more than a leader; it takes someone who dares to play, transform, and go beyond leadership. When we dare to play, we no longer seek to follow others; instead, we take charge of our choices. When we dare to play, we recognize that play and joy are essential to our humanity. Chapter 4 introduced the different play archetypes and talked about ways adults enter into play. Leaders can use this information as we design opportunities for adult play. Knowing how people enter and engage in play is the beginning of leading with playfulness in mind.

In the field of early childhood education, we are perennially discussing what is best for young children. We hear that universal preschool is the answer to help children living in historically excluded and underresourced areas, especially Black, Indigenous, and other children of color. We have followed the message that more academics are better for children who live in these situations. But our thinking is biased when we believe that children who live in poverty need different preparation than children from higher-income households. When we dare to play, we learn that joy is more important than preparing children for the next stage in their life. We transform ourselves into educators who recognize the innate need children have to play and, hopefully, stop focusing on standardized education.

Many of us have adopted the idea of "readying" children for kindergarten. We may have started implementing curricula that promise to be research-based or pushed for academics at the expense of play. We support this idea of more academics because we believe the leaders who push this concept know more than we do. They have convinced us that having more academics at an earlier age will help children succeed later in life. After all, they claim that their practices are research-based without acknowledging that the research might not necessarily lead to the conclusion they are stating. In other words, we follow orders without questioning them. Rather, it is our responsibility to know and analyze the research and not take at face value what is being said to us. Often people believe that a leader is someone who has many followers. But merely having followers does not make a good leader. The people who implement these academic practices think they know more than the average educator. They have used their power to have more followers. But a true leader listens to and respects diverse perspectives. An effective leader invites stakeholders to work together and find the best solutions in individual communities with unique needs. We are now beginning to see that transitional kindergarten and universal preschool programs often have not produced the practical results they promised (Durkin et al. 2022). As a profession, it is time we start questioning the leaders we follow. Since the publication of this peer-reviewed article, there have been multiple analyses and responses to the report. Many have used the study to justify how their practices are different and effective. I offer a word of warning from a leadership perspective. As a profession, we must never follow. We must make our work representative of the community we live in.

Leaders know that they do not have all the answers, and they know that when people come together, social justice and change become possible. Leadership emerges from social influence and not the assertion of authority or power. Leadership engages others to support the common goal. A leader may have different attitudes, approaches, or styles of leading. However, they know that their approach is not the final voice. A leader aims for the common goal, not trying to influence others to think the same way as they do or follow them without thinking. Leadership is about maximizing the efforts and voices of people to solve a problem or create an innovative solution to support society. An empathic leader does not say, "Do you see the problem? Follow me, and I will guide you to find the solution." Instead, a leader will say, "You see the problems; let's come together to find a solution."

I also encourage you to come to your own definition of *leadership* so that it matches your values and is clearly instilled in your attitude and how you approach life.

Dream and Play

We must dare to dream beyond current expectations and make our vision visible to others. Playful leaders understand that dreaming and questioning can inspire change. They know how to create a culture where people can ask questions that may disrupt the status quo. A playful and transformational attitude creates a culture where people can dream about their personal and professional lives and invest in supporting their dreams. Leaders place resources and energy in dreaming and making their dreams visible and reachable. In education we are experiencing burnout, and many are exiting the profession. Helping people achieve their goals and remain playful and creative can help prevent burnout and retain educators. Dreaming is essential, and even more crucial is giving people the opportunity to make their dreams become a reality.

Play is a basic need for humans. We thrive when we play and are more capable of developing innovative ideas. When we combine play and leadership, we can create a culture that invites people to find joy in their work. Playful leadership understands that work is not just about meeting standards and completing mountains of paperwork. Instead, playful leaders recognize that we must always nurture a playful attitude. When we dare to play, we begin to create a culture where play is a mindset and an essential part of every aspect of daily work, from interactions with people to the way we set up the early childhood ecosystem to invite play. Children benefit when adults play and embrace a playful mood; adults respect children's education by allowing ample time for and valuing child-initiated and child-centered play.

Playfulness is the best motivator to create spaces that bring joy to our lives. Playfulness can happen even when we do ongoing tasks, from completing paperwork to brainstorming to running a meeting. A playful mindset is relaxed, creative, imaginative, and in a constant state of flow. A playful ecosystem does not create competition that focuses ruthlessly on increasing performance. Instead, it goes beyond praise and competition to create a place of inclusion and brings equity into work and life. When we combine play and leadership, we realize that we can meet work demands with an attitude that increases productivity and engagement.

● JUST PLAY! CHALLENGE ●

A PLAY ON CRAFT STICKS

Begin by gathering craft sticks that have a surface that can be used for writing. You need six different colors, one of which is natural/uncolored, with a minimum of five per color per participant. You will also need black fine-point permanent markers. A selection of neutral-colored blocks can enhance the construction process as well.

Step 1: Introduce the exploration to the group: "As we move forward to create a culture of synergy and playfulness, we must uncover which values mean the most to us, both individually and as an organization. This exploration will help evaluate your own and the collective values of the program. As we use the craft sticks to play, our values will become clearer. Let's explore the values that we want to influence our thoughts, emotions, and behaviors."

Step 2: Distribute the craft sticks to each participant, five of each color, for a total of thirty craft sticks each. Ask participants to spread out the craft sticks in front of them so they can see each stick.

Step 3: Pick the first color (e.g., red). Ask each participant to write down five objects that they need to function every day, one item on each of the red craft sticks. Some examples are cell phones, cars, food, water, shelter, and so on.

Step 4: Pick the second color (e.g., blue). Ask participants to write down on each of their blue craft sticks a geographical location that is important to them. It could be their family home, a place where they have traveled, a place where they grew up, or a place where they work or volunteer.

Step 5: Pick the third color (e.g., yellow). Ask participants to write down on each of the yellow craft sticks the name of a person who has contributed to their life and influenced who they are today. Remind participants that this person could have had a positive or negative influence.

Step 6: Pick the fourth color (e.g., orange). Ask participants to write on each of the orange craft sticks a personal or professional goal (short or long term).

Step 7: Pick the fifth color (e.g., purple). Ask participants to write down on each of the purple craft sticks a significant memory that they always want to hold close.

Step 8: Ask participants to write one value (creativity, empathy, vulnerability, humbleness, and so forth) on each of the five natural-color craft sticks.

Step 9: Once everyone has finished writing, ask participants to take a few moments to silently read over their blocks and make changes if they like. (Provide spare craft sticks as needed for revisions.)

Step 10: Ask participants to rearrange their colored craft sticks under each of their five values (the uncolored craft sticks). At this point, they can leave some of the items that do not fit into the specific values to the side. This part of the exploration helps people focus on their values and what they really need to support each value. It is an eye-opening exploration that recenters people to renegotiate their personal values.

I know you are probably asking where the play is in this process. So, here it comes.

Step 11: Ask participants to pick one craft stick of each color (not including the uncolored craft sticks) and share what they wrote. Once they have shared, they can come to the front and place it on a table, together building a tall craft stick structure (focus on height). You can add neutral-colored blocks to facilitate the construction. Repeat this exercise until every craft stick is used. At this point, the structure is probably fairly tall and perhaps unbalanced or maybe has fallen a few times.

Step 12: Ask participants to share their five values (written on the uncolored craft sticks) and place them in a separate structure.

Step 13: It is likely that common threads have surfaced as everyone shared. Invite participants to deconstruct and then rebuild the structure. Discuss what they want to keep and what they can eliminate. What happens when items are taken away? What else needs to be added to keep the structure balanced? At this point, suggest that the value structure be merged into the main structure. Have an open discussion about which values should be included in the structure, and, hence, in the organization. Be inclusive and come to consensus when a value is chosen. Be sensitive to the fact that some values will be eliminated, and they had meaning to the person who wrote them. Ask if any values are missing, and give the group another chance to include them by writing them on a spare uncolored craft stick.

Consider gluing the tower together to remind everyone about their work and the agreements they reached about the values that guide their practices.

CREATING A DREAM TOWER

This is similar to the Play on Craft Sticks exploration but with a focus on dreams. Distribute craft sticks, starting with one per participant. Invite participants to write one word that describes a personal dream on a craft stick. Invite them to share their dream. Ask them to share what would make the dream happen. Ask them to write a short answer on the back side of the stick. They can take notes on a separate piece of paper if needed. Ask if they would like input from colleagues. If they say yes, ask each colleague to write a short response on a different craft stick.

In the end, each participant will have created an individual dream craft stick. Invite the group to build a structure using everyone's sticks, and let them know that they can continue to build and add to the tower or structure as each new step toward the dream has been achieved.

Remind participants that this is both personal and collective work. Each member of the team is invested in supporting the others to achieve their dreams.

Creating a Playful Culture

Although it is clear that meeting people's basic needs is necessary so they can grow as humans, I am concerned that we spend so much time meeting people's needs (including our own) that we lose sight of the incredible strengths they have to contribute to solutions and change their lives. Happily, these strengths naturally emerge during play. When we dare to play, we focus on regeneration and self-realization every day and create sustainable change. Leaders must acquire and demonstrate the following characteristics to create a culture that promotes playfulness.

Observe and Listen

Start with being a keen observer of human behavior. Take time every day to practice observing. Take notes of what you see. Focus on people's strengths instead of looking for what you think they need. When we assume that there are needs, we are using a "power over" lens, but when we look for strengths, we build relationships where power is shared. Notice how people express themselves, how they use their body language, how they communicate their thinking, and how they interact with others. Notice the strengths educators have and plan how to support them. Observe how they solve problems and how they implement innovative practices. Watch for their playfulness as they interact with children and other adults.

Keep a list of the strengths you see and be ready to share them at meetings. Invite educators to further explore the list. Keep in mind that these strengths can also be shared slowly and informally. Invite educators to identify one another's strengths, and consider keeping an ongoing list in the educators' lounge. When we focus on strengths, solving problems is easier.

Lead with Love

As humans, we need to be loved with all our flaws, and we want the opportunity to love others back. When we create a space centered on valuing and respecting play, people feel loved and accepted and may be more willing to be part of the community.

Build Relationships

As leaders, we need to ensure that people trust one another and feel comfortable being their authentic selves. A playful environment loosens tension and sends the message that we can handle difficult situations together because we are in a safe and loving relationship. Playful leaders value people and know how important it is for colleagues to connect with one another. Play is a great connector because it requires authenticity and vulnerability. Just like children, when adults play, they enter into a safe space where they can trust one another.

Playful leadership requires tremendous social intelligence to know when a gentle, funny comment during an intense discussion can bring out smiles and shift everyone back into that safe, loving space. A playful leader listens in appreciation, asks questions fueled by sincere curiosity, tells personal stories, and is willing to laugh. In other words, playful leaders are not afraid to be imperfect. They know that they are human and care for the humanity of people. Playful leaders openly and unapologetically show their passion for play, and they share their passion by inviting others to join them.

Lead with Empathy

An effective playful leader is grounded in empathy and compassion and is attuned to people's moods. They seek to understand how these moods affect the chemistry and interactions within a community. When an ecosystem's community embraces playfulness, people interact with positive intent. This is because the people's interactions come from a more playful and supportive perspective. When love and positive intent are the base of the community interactions, people are more willing to develop a genuine interest in fostering positive feelings in themselves and others.

Increase Sensitivity

Being able to understand and respond to people's way of being in the world is an essential characteristic of a leader. Seek to read people's cues and reactions. Scan the room and notice where people sit. Do they make eye contact with one another? Are they in specific groups, or are they keeping a distance? Do they nod or shake their heads when someone is speaking?

In other words, heighten your awareness of every movement and reaction so that you get feedback you may use to better engage people. Being a keen observer and being aware of your own reactions helps you develop a deep capacity to channel your focus with precision, make thoughtful choices, and spark rich insights to create a play culture that builds the capacity for creativity and innovation.

Think Soundly

Thinking soundly requires us to recognize our patterns of thought and pay attention to how they guide our practices. For example, when we confront a problem, do we first feel despair, or do we playfully approach it as an opportunity to grow? I once tended to see problems as something overwhelming and unsurmountable. I now play with problems to explore possible answers. Sometimes I play with diagrams or graphs. Other times I just paint and let my brain flow. By the end of the playtime, I have a better perspective on the problem and I can begin to find solutions. I have learned that the connections we make with our thinking patterns also affect the people we lead, so I play freely and frequently to help ensure that our collective thinking patterns are playful and joyful.

Always Be Curious

We are born to be inquisitive. Unfortunately, somewhere down the line, many of us lose our instinct for curiosity. Curiosity is a critical leadership skill for creating transformative growth and change. It is also closely linked to the development of relationships. When we are curious, we want to listen to and understand the people close to us. Be bold, ask questions, and create multiple opportunities to explore your curiosity. Challenge yourself to do something new. Ask yourself, "What I am curious about today?" and pursue that daily curiosity. For instance, sometimes when I listen to a podcast I hear something that sparks my curiosity and becomes my guide to play that day. I research, I read, I have a conversation with friends, or I simply explore my curiosity in play. I invite you to let your curiosity guide your play.

Always Wonder

Cultivate a sense of wonder and awe. Step into every situation wondering what new learning will come your way. Many of us spend a lot of time wishing and little time wondering. For instance, "I wish I could play more" is just a wish with no action. But "I wonder how I can play more" sets me into action. I can make a plan and take the first steps. As leaders, when we encourage wonderment, we give ourselves and our colleagues an effective way to handle their professional and personal lives. Wondering helps us drop our need for control and become curious, more open to the flow of life.

Use Experimental-Mindedness

When we are open to experimenting with new ideas, concepts, or processes, we create a culture that sees mistakes as opportunities for growth. Experimentation requires inclusivity and equity of voice. Leaders who are open to new perspectives and are willing to leave their egos at the door can increase joyfulness, playfulness, creativity, and innovative thinking. An experimental-minded leader recognizes that they do not have all the answers. Instead, they invite people to lead with questions, test their theories, and find answers together. In other words, everyone can "fail forward and fail fast" and learn by doing. We will sometimes fail, but when failure is recognized as an opportunity to redirect, we are more motivated to experiment with new ideas and stop doing the same thing over and over without different results.

For instance, a simple way to celebrate mistakes is to start meetings with a Jamboree of Failure. Start by sharing a prop that symbolizes a mistake. Invite people to bring items that represent their mistakes too. I like to use a piece of jewelry I made that was the result of a mistake but became an exciting piece that I wear often. Participants take brief turns sharing their experiences, including the context of the experience, what happened, what innovative solution they came up with, and what they learned from the mistake.

Have a Sense of Humor

Our sense of humor is closely related to our humanity. A sense of humor is how we perceive the world, keep our sanity, and remain human, responsive, and playful. Leading with a sense of humor helps us build relationships and gain likability. A sense of humor minimizes status hierarchy and diffuses tension. Having a sense of humor does a lot to develop a playful attitude. When we laugh together and share a moment of playfulness, we build community. With a sense of humor, we are present in the moment with the people in the room.

Be Flexible

Flexibility can help leaders adapt to and maneuver in difficult moments with joy and a playful attitude. Having the flexibility to switch between tasks can act as a palette cleanser, spark creativity and motivation, and reduce burnout. When leaders create a variety of types of playfulness in all interactions, it promotes everyone's sense of agency and ownership.

Develop Compassionate Leadership

With so many educators exiting the profession, compassionate leadership is a must. A playful leader's work is centered on people before outcomes. Play motivates the heart and brings joy to an ecosystem. When a leader commits to creating a playful culture, they lead with compassion and understanding. They model being present and delight in the precious playful moments that happen every day.

Learn How to Learn

The world is constantly changing, and we exist in a state of flux. What keeps us moving forward is our capacity to learn and learn fast. A playful leader is a keen and effective learner who embraces instability with creative thinking. When we know how to learn, we can discover answers to satisfy our curiosity.

Choosing Playfulness

Playfulness is a choice we make. We can choose to see opportunities and possibilities in every challenge. When we embrace play, our freedom to explore increases, and we are more open to test multiple ideas and solutions. We turn our challenges into play—through joking, using our imaginations, or exploring solutions with a lighthearted attitude.

A culture of playfulness takes into consideration multiple perspectives instead of focusing on narrow, arbitrary goals. As a leader, are you ready to make a change? When we engage in playful leadership, we benefit in many ways:

- We build better relationships and stronger collaborations. Play allows us to be more vulnerable and intimate. Playfulness helps us make new connections with people and strengthen existing relationships by making them more meaningful.

- Playfulness outcompetes anxiety. We need to train our brains to pause and redirect our thoughts to be more positive. This is where play comes in, nudging us away from the negative.

- Play relieves stress. Playful activities engage our minds rather than numb them. Drawing, painting, making a video, playing a board game, creating a playlist, role-playing with friends, or going on an adventure can help lessen anxiety by bringing joy into our daily lives.

- Play expands our horizons. When we play, we see things in new ways. Seeing connections between things that appear unrelated is the hallmark of creativity. Too often we look at situations the same way. For instance, we might use the same educational themes every year or follow the same schedule even when we know it is not working. Play allows us to see the world with a fresh outlook.

- Play offers the opportunity to exercise both analytical and creative thinking at the same time. It helps us think *without* the box.

Remember that a culture of playfulness will increase creativity, morale, and innovation because different perspectives are honored. Dare to play and transform.

● JUST PLAY! CHALLENGE ●

Shift meetings and conversations to center on playfulness and creative thinking. At your next meeting, share a play memory of your childhood. Bring the artifacts that inspired the play. For instance, if you share how you used rocks to build imaginary worlds, bring rocks for people to create their own imaginary worlds. Next meeting, invite people to bring their play memories and the artifacts that inspired them. Spend the rest of the time playing. You can continue revisiting the memories by placing the artifacts in different ecosystem areas.

Start a meeting with an exploration of the various toys currently in the ecosystem. Explore them, make connections to each item, and think about how the toys support your play and young children's play.

Invite educators to try different art media or set up an area for water play. Water and art are playful and calming. Make Zen garden trays available for sand and design play, include fidgets for educators to play with during meetings, and encourage doodling by providing butcher paper and markers.

When a task is too much to accomplish alone, break tasks into steps, divide participants into groups, and invite educators to explore different solutions.

Let them know that no idea is off limits and that playfulness must guide the process. It may be helpful to turn each task into a mystery game or a case study to solve. Give educators creative materials (paint, markers, drawing tools, and Loose Parts) to explore the task.

Learn from TikTok. Social media platform TikTok has become such a phenomenon because it delivers high-energy and engaging content in small, bite-sized videos. These videos are often funny, inspiring, and engaging. Take cues from TikTok and make meeting content short and epic. Start with a question, such as, "If you were trying to make cleanup time fun and enjoyable, what would you do?" Generate as many ideas as possible. The ideas can be silly, unusable, complicated, or impossible. Ask that participants prepare as a group a one-minute presentation of their idea. They can make a video, draw it, sing it, or act it out. Once every idea is presented, decide as a group which idea(s) to prototype, test, and analyze.

Variation: Encourage participants to build on one another's ideas. TikTok has a stitching feature that allows users to create content by adding their own video to an original video. You can also do the same by combining two ideas together into one presentation. Think of this as assembling a crazy quilt with multiple blocks contributing to the whole.

Design games that create an inviting and inclusive atmosphere. Make a "Guess Who" game for discussing play archetypes. For example:

Guess Who: Who are the people who enjoy telling jokes or playing harmless pranks?

Answer: The humorous archetype

Guess Who: This archetype seeks the adrenaline rush of contests, rivalries, and face-offs. They play games with rules, keep score, and strive to win the final prize.

Answer: The competitor archetype

Ask people to identify their play archetypes. Remind them that they can have multiple archetypes.

Reflections

- How does using the archetypes enhance your playful leadership abilities?

- What strategies will you use to embrace the qualities of a playful leader?

- How will you create an ecosystem that embraces playfulness and brings joy?

CHAPTER 6

Playful Professional Development

The very ordinariness of playing has immense
affective and life-enhancing significance.

—Stuart Lester

So much professional development is available for educators, administrators, and staff, but very little is focused on engaging creativity and playfulness. Many educators have shared with me their experiences of repetitive, monotonous, or disengaging workshops. It's exhausting and dispiriting. Perhaps it is time to change the way we deliver professional development. We want to engage creativity, retain educators' passion, and increase job satisfaction. Professional development can help educators learn the required knowledge and meet expectations while still developing a playful attitude and finding joy.

Playful experiences help people commit to their role as learners. When people play, they increase their cognitive skills, such as awareness, problem solving, and communication. As early childhood education continues to evolve, so too must our professional development, organizational culture, and values. What motivates current educators is also changing, as they are increasingly digital natives inspired by empowerment, trust, instant feedback, and flexibility. As a result, we must develop proactive and creative strategies for learning with play-based activities that allow educators to experiment and explore in a supportive environment. By embracing change and encouraging creativity, workshops can meet the needs of today's educators.

When I talk to educators, I get a sense of sadness. Their job seems overwhelming, and they are not hopeful about the future. I recently presented to a group of educators, and the staff from one specific school spent the entire time laughing and mocking what I was saying. Their image of children was so negative that they could not engage their creativity. This was a cultural situation that had been present in this group for a long time. My strategy was to allow them to continue to play with Loose Parts throughout the presentation. I just came around and asked a few questions to help them get out of their negative frame of mind. I knew that I could not make a huge difference in their thinking with one presentation, but I also know that playful leadership can go a long way in changing negative cultures at work.

Imagine entering a room, dreading another dry professional development workshop. However, the workshop facilitator welcomes you personally and asks a few questions to connect and get to know you better. You look around the room and notice that every table has different Loose Parts. The facilitator encourages you to walk around and touch the different materials. Calming music is playing in the background. As you continue to look around the room, you notice photographs of adults and children playing. Easel paper and markers are arranged in beautiful containers and strategically placed around the room. A beautiful natural smell permeates the environment. Soon the music shifts to something more upbeat, inviting you to dance. You begin to let go of your inhibitions, and you are now ready to play. The space is designed to get you in the flow, engage your whole person, and find your creativity.

This is just one example of what professional development can look like. The focus is not just on learning new licensing requirements or specific outcomes. Instead, the focus is on helping educators connect with play. Once they find their joy, they are more ready to learn about the specific requirements of a program. This chapter takes a different look at professional development and creates a "yes/and" attitude, proving that you can bring a more playful attitude and still get the business part of work done.

● JUST PLAY! CHALLENGE ●

Invite the team to play a game in which they look at a situation as a crisis or a total disaster. For example, think about one uncontrollable child who likes to throw everything and scream. Ask them to reflect on what would happen if they don't solve the challenge, including the consequences for children and for themselves. They can role-play, draw, or create a collage. An exercise such as this one can help shift people's thinking out of a negative frame in which they see every situation as unsolvable. It opens the door to engage in more creative thinking and helps people realize that every *no* can lead to a *yes*.

Start each meeting with a drumming or clapping circle to create a trusting rhythm in the organization. One person starts the rhythm, and the next person in the circle extends the set with a new sequence. After each person introduces their sequence, the group can continue to take turns or combine the sequences and play them at the same time. The idea is to get into a rhythm that feels comfortable and engaging.

Try bringing back childhood hand-clapping games. Played in groups of four, Rockin' Robin is one fun example set to the tune of the popular 1958 song by singer Bobby Day.

Redefining Professional
Development through Play

As I conducted research for this book, I took a deep dive into reviewing and analyzing the current professional development offerings. They appeared to self-organize into the following categories:

- Specific content (for example, teaching math, science, language and literacy, and so on)

- Child development and learning

- Observation and assessment

- Culture, diversity, and equity

- Inclusion

- Early childhood quality improvement

- Childhood trauma

- Family engagement

- Guided play

- Challenging behaviors and guidance

Evidence exists that play supports learning, even in adults, yet we rarely use play to promote a playful attitude in educators. Play is filled with lessons to be learned. When learning isn't fun, the lessons can all too easily diminish understanding and leave adults doubting their capacities. When playfulness is incorporated into the learning process and the focus shifts to the process instead of just delivering a product, the opportunities for collaboration and authentic relationship building increase, and everyone's true learning and understanding are enhanced.

Our profession has not been consistent in defending play as an intrinsic need and right of all human beings. We keep saying that play is learning, but we have failed in making clear connections. As you begin to shift professional development to be more playful, it is essential to demonstrate *how* play is learning by making each outcome visible. Fortunately, the task is not that complicated. We just need to create more opportunities to play and center our learning on joy and pleasure. When educators embrace play and playfulness, they enter the world of "what if" as they reflect on possible futures, values, perspectives, needs, interests, and choices. Through this playful reflective process, they begin to identify challenges, redefine roles, and closely articulate differences and similarities in thinking, ideas, and perspectives. This process is not unlike design thinking or scientific thinking. Playfulness enables liberation in learning because it connects to alertness and intellectual curiosity.

As I present around the country, I often have educators ask me how they can connect play to learning outcomes. Many times, their constant need to prove how play helps children learn has limited their own ability to embrace it. At the end of a presentation on the power of play, one of the participants, with tears in her eyes, said, "This is the first time I played as an adult, and I now know the value and importance of letting children play." Of course, my heart was whole.

Planning a Playful Professional Development Session

One of the goals of playful professional development is to invite educators to challenge their own boundaries and their current thinking, which requires us to provide opportunities for everyone to make mistakes, take risks, and explore innovative ways of learning. The idea is to disrupt the process of traditional professional development and instead play to learn and to make sustainable change. I have learned that the more time I spend planning and playing with every concept, the more successful my presentation will be. With this goal in mind, I begin the process of planning a presentation. I ask myself questions:

- How will I make current professional development more playful?

- How will I include each play archetype so that participants are engaged and participate joyfully?

- How will I recognize participants who are having a difficult time engaging in play, and what will I do to make them feel comfortable?

- How will I incorporate the learning through play?

- What supporting tools and materials will I need?

As I plan a presentation, I consider how I played as a child and think about the playful moments I remember the most. I represent them by sketching or collaging. Some of my fondest memories of playing as a child came as I created complex imaginary worlds. I had a playhouse where I spent a lot of time pretending to cook and hosting tea parties. The house also served as a club where I gathered with my neighborhood friends to plan new adventures. The house was a safe place where we could play alone without adult intervention. We did argue and fight, but we always found ways to solve our disputes and continue to play together. I am still friends with many of my childhood neighbors. The playful and warm feelings that still emanate from my childhood are replicated in most of my professional development presentations. I focus on the following elements:

- Safety (including physical, social, emotional, and cognitive safety): Creating a space of trust that allows for risk-taking.

- Relationships: Building relationships based on trust.

- Disrupting the status quo: Creating adventures that help us think outside (or better yet, without) the box.

- Playfulness and joy: Eliciting a sense of joy and unapologetic playfulness.

Once I have a clear image of those moments, I ask myself, "How can I create the conditions for educators to explore their playfulness? What type of active explorations can I offer for them to discover joy? What cultural values do my participants have? What opportunities to play did they have as children? What is the general culture of the agency or program?" Likewise, you can plan for play by sending a questionnaire to the organizers or participants ahead of time. Even with this preparation you may not get all the answers you need, so be prepared to offer multiple ways to engage the audience.

From informal surveys I have conducted at presentations, I know that one of the common trends of play experiences is memories of playing outdoors. So I make sure that outdoor play is included when possible, or I bring in natural Loose Parts.

To design the professional development day, I start by creating a simple outline. The day's outline is based on how a story is told, with a beginning, a middle, and an end. Weaving a story through the day helps me see the continuity, rhythm, and purpose of the presentation.

When possible, I visit the space in advance. I consider how people will move in the space and how they will engage with one another. I consider how I can make it a welcome space where ideas, thoughts, prototyping, and testing naturally emerge. I integrate Loose Parts and other tools that invite wonderment and creativity. For example, I like to provide acrylic shapes in a variety of colors for a color exploration. They can be combined with different paint media to increase interest. Frequently, I set up tables like these, chosen for their aesthetic value and ability to spark inspiration:

- A table with intentionally curated Loose Parts
- A table with collage materials
- A table with different paint media
- A table with clay and clay tools

When I conduct larger professional development workshops, I bring baskets containing the materials and invite educators to select the basket they want to use. I make sure many active explorations are woven into the presentation or workshop. People need to play with words, concepts, and ideas to make meaning of what they are learning.

JUST PLAY! CHALLENGE

Start a professional development session with a simple twist to the classic telephone game. People sit in a circle. One person is asked to start by sharing a phrase that includes a value they believe in. For example, "I value play because it brings me joy." Participants whisper the phrase to each other, going around the circle, until the last person shares the phrase out loud. Follow the activity with a discussion that explores how listening is a skill that begins with being present.

Use the word *playful* to identify ways that help participants feel a sense of belonging. For example, start by listing *P* words that help you feel welcome:

Powerful	Precious	Positive	Present
Plenitude	Personal	Possessions	

Depending on the number of participants, you can divide into groups to explore specific letters. To make the interaction more playful, I provide a wide variety of Loose Parts so participants can represent how they would integrate each word into their early childhood ecosystems. You can also provide art tools.

When I explore social media, I often see adults posing next to a sculpture or artwork, re-creating its pose. To me, adults' need to re-create what they see is closely related to the need to play. Let us bring this sense of wonder and play into professional development. Select a series of artworks that include people and have them enlarged. Place them throughout the room and invite educators to walk around and analyze each painting for its beauty, color, symmetry, and balance. Have them take notes and write down as many details as they can.

After they all have explored each artwork, divide them into small groups (three to four people). Give each group a copy of one of the works and ask them not to share which one it is as they re-create it by becoming human statues. The rest of the groups guess which work they are re-creating.

Take a different spin on this playful exploration by re-creating something you see in nature. For example, use your body to represent the branches of a tree, move to the rhythm of the wind, or fly with the elegant movements of a bird.

When we actively use our bodies and our senses, we become more aware of the details we see and how we feel. When we gain awareness, we begin to value the power of observing and supporting children's investigations. We can then begin to change our ecosystems and fill the "in-between" gaps with more meaningful moments of play.

Start every meeting with a dance. It can be open dancing, or you can teach one another different types of dancing. I love flamenco, so before conferences and professional development meetings, a friend and I sometimes start with a few flamenco moves and invite others to join. Bring scarves and ribbons to help people engage in movement. Play music with a variety of rhythms and sounds.

When a meeting is intense, invite participants outside for a friendly tug-of-war game. You will see how the competition shifts the dynamics of the meeting. Often the healthy diversion allows participants to be more innovative.

Incorporate movement into the mental work of brainstorming and harnessing the hive mind by giving educators paint suits and inviting them to write their ideas on one another. Create a road map educators can move through physically by using large Loose Parts (tunnels, hula hoops, boxes, ramps, and large unit blocks).

Ask yourself: How will my thinking shift as I incorporate more playfulness into my work?

The Power of Improvisation

One technique I have learned over the years of designing playful professional development is that adding improvisation activities can invite educators to play. When educators play together, we strengthen our relationships with fellow colleagues. Through improvisation we cocreate a world that invites us to speculate, go beyond the limits, rationalities, and everyday challenges of the "real" world and collaborate. We may use the toolset of improv to explore different ways of thinking. In other words, we can imagine what *more* might be possible.

Every time I watch the classic television show *Whose Line Is It Anyway?* I marvel at how responsive each comedian is to the others' ideas and representations. It takes an incredible amount of observation, understanding, and imagination to create a well-coordinated spontaneous moment. During improv sequences, people make offers or invitations for others to join. These invitations are the material with which improvised scenes are created. They require us to carefully listen and observe body cues. An offer or invitation is anything that anyone says or does in a story or scene. The rules of improvisation require that all invitations are accepted. No one is allowed to pass. Instead, we respond, saying, "Yes, and . . ." The idea of "Yes, and" speaks to me because it brings forth opportunities rather than challenges. When we respond with "Yes, and," we are open to the possibility of growth and engagement.

These improvisational moments are not much different from the way children play. When children engage in pretend or fantasy play, they often create a complex script that can be difficult to follow. They move fast and exchange dialogue that might seem to adults to be unconnected. However, you can see the repetition of topics they are exploring, the nonverbal cues, coordinated movement, and use of objects to represent their thinking.

In the book *Pretend Play as Improvisation: Conversation in the Preschool Classroom*, Dr. Robert Keith Sawyer offers a comparison between improvisation and children's pretend play. He conducted a yearlong ethnographical study of children's play in a kindergarten class. In this study, he found that children's play closely resembles the collaborative performance of improvisation troupes. Sawyer argues that when participating in theatrical improvisation, adults are responsive and begin to respond with a "Yes, and" attitude. Improv requires that the players work together rather than focusing on their own ideas, goals, or egos. It assumes a commitment to the whole rather than a focus on the particular. Just like children's pretend play, an improv troupe works together to create a well-orchestrated dialogue. Just like children's play, an improvised scene uses every suggestion and every mistake and transforms them into a cohesive whole (Sawyer 1997).

Play the "Yes, and" improv game to create a story together. The first person starts with a statement, such as "Last night, I went to a friend's house." The next person continues the story by starting with the sentence, "Yes, and I trust he is recuperating well after his surgery?" Each person adds a new sentence, and each sentence begins with the words "Yes, and." The "yes" signifies that the person has heard everything that came before and accepts that it is real. The "and" directs each person to add a little something of their own.

Playing this game can shed light on how we engage in collective activities. When a story flows and the meaning is clear, you can tell every participant is completely attuned to the story. When the responses to the invitations are random, you can identify which participants are not working collectively. This can lead to a conversation about how being fully present enhances relationships with children and colleagues.

Here are more ideas for facilitating improv:

● Introduce a specific idea, object, or challenge to get the game started.

● Remind participants not to overthink the game but just to listen and continue the story.

● Keep the ideas going. If someone needs help, who can step in with a suggestion?

Ask yourself: What did I discover after participating in the "Yes, and" game? How did the group collectively engage in the "Yes, and" game? What connections do I make to children's play and my role as a player? What was challenging/interesting about this activity? When I use the "Yes, and" approach in my work, how does it help me shift my current practices?

Getting comfortable with improv games helps educators observe children's play sequences and recognize how they can become part of the play without changing it. After every play experience and every improv game, stop to analyze and reflect on what was learned and make connections to the power of play:

Listening and observing. Listening to one another and watching body cues, as practiced in improv, is crucial when working with children. Educators need to be present and ready to step in when a child asks for help. Yet educators must control the urge to step in, and when stepping in is warranted they must figure out how to participate without changing the purpose of the game. The more educators are attuned to the organic play process, the more they can create the conditions to facilitate and respect children's play.

Working collectively. As educators work together to create an improv story, they recognize that if one individual attempts to fit the story to their agenda only, the story is no longer a collective effort and the flow is disrupted. Likewise, when we enter children's play with our adult agenda, we change their interactions. Actively accepting other people's offers allows us to go on a journey alongside them.

Avoiding negation. Negating is the opposite of accepting invitations. When people negate, they deny what has come before; for example, saying, "I have never visited a place with snow, so I do not know what to do." Commonly, when someone is not happy with the story's path, they will attempt to change it with a negation. Eventually, as people continue to work with improv, they learn to see gaps in the collective synergy and shift to create a more cohesive story. As educators continue playing improv games, they develop their ability to recognize when they are negating children's ideas and interests. When we consider "true play," or the play that originates from children and is led by children, we know that the play is richer without adults redirecting or interrupting. Educators often have an idea of what play should be, and they may be tempted to guide the play to teach a particular concept. However, to support children's play, educators need to recognize when their agenda is determining the play's direction and instead accept the children's invitations.

Taking responsibility for the group. In improv, you must listen to what other people are adding to the story. Listening to what is missing is also essential. Sometimes the story in a "Yes, and" game is going nowhere, and someone has to step forward to keep the improv story moving, without controlling the outcome. Likewise, educators facilitating children's play must remain attuned to what the group is doing. While educators must be cautious not to take over, they can make offers that spark children's ideas.

Taking risks. When educators engage in improvisation, they take a safe risk. They are in a space where there is no right or wrong. Educators benefit from the lack of judgment and may begin to take more risks in the classroom. They may become more open to experimentation and unscripted exploration. Children's play is often risky and exciting. However, at times it makes educators uncomfortable. Recognizing the importance of taking risks can help educators create the conditions where children can engage in more complex play and richer possibilities, ultimately to make sense in their lives. This includes shifting from expecting children to know how to behave or "know better" what is expected of them.

Improv activities can invite more playfulness and challenge educators to use more risk-taking, creativity, and innovation. You may at this point be asking, "How do I facilitate improv games if I have not been part of an improv troupe?" Many resources are available to help you: Improv facilitators can be hired for events. Books offer ideas for improv games and teach you how to facilitate them. What is important is to value the power of play and bring it to educators in your programs.

Reflections

- What memories have motivated you to learn something new, and how will you use the memories to design playful professional development?

- What strategies will you use to make professional development more playful and meaningful?

- How will you increase your capacities to observe and support others' strengths?

CHAPTER 7

Just Play! Conferences

Surrendering to the unknown can be hard, if not
impossible, for me. Oh sure, I'm a free spirit. I break into
song. I get a groove on when Motown pops into my
head in the middle of a keynote to five hundred people.
I travel the world. I meet new people to love every day.

—Holly Elissa Bruno, *The Comfort of Little Things*

Imagine walking the streets in downtown Las Vegas in the middle of summer, and instead of the typical desert scene, you find yourself in the middle
of a winter wonderland. There are places to ice-skate, have a snowball fight,
admire the winter lights, and drink cocktails reminiscent of a winter vil-
lage. Musicians are playing enchanting music, and you get lost, in awe of
the scenery and illusion. I once experienced this when I attended a conference catering to the entertainment industry. I left that moment inspired
and with a sense of wonder that lasted for a long time. Of course, I do not

propose to compete with the movie studios, which have the resources and finances to create any scene anywhere. But I do suggest that we design conferences that inspire and get educators in a state of wonderment.

In my years working in early childhood education, community organizing, and family development, I have attended many conferences and participated in many institutes with a large group of people in attendance. It seems that these meetings are all organized in a similar format. They start with a pre-institute session that focuses on a specific topic (often to inform the profession on the new mandates or policies). A keynote presentation designed to inspire and motivate attendees opens the main conference. Then follows a series of presentations preselected by a panel of reviewers.

When I walk around, I notice that the presentations that attract the most people have music, storytelling, puppetry, play, or other interactive components. I remember attending Bev Bos's workshops. She and Michael Leeman had the natural ability to entertain, engage, and inspire people while imparting deep knowledge. They would have us up and moving and talking to one another. Bev would read her new favorite book to us, and then we played with concepts, words, and ideas. I always left wanting more.

When I attend the national conferences, I often skip the workshops and presentations and just spend my time meeting people and networking. When I visit the exhibitors' area, it is apparent that educators enjoy engaging in the games and treasure hunts organized by the companies. Of course, the games and gimmicks are designed to encourage people to purchase their products. After a while, I tend to find the noise level so high that I exit the exhibit hall to find a place for a moment of quiet refuge. The noise, the crowds, and the ongoing blinking lights can get exhausting. Yet the experience gets participants engaged as they look for freebies and swag they can take home. I guess we can consider these interactions a form of playful engagement. I wonder if it promotes a playful attitude that lasts long.

I know that by attending conferences I have met some remarkable people and forged friendships that have made my life better. I hope that conferences will someday offer more opportunities to help us let go of our inhibitions and embrace a more playful attitude. In this chapter, I propose some elements to incorporate play into conferences.

One of the best conferences I ever attended was the Good Stuff for Kids Conference organized by Roseville [California] Community Preschool. We convened for three full days of inspiring speakers, delightful play explorations, and evenings of music that touched the heart. We played together, shared stories, and asked questions. The conference was designed to engage adults in play and wonderment, from labyrinths (made with shoes forming the maze borders) to sensory experiences where we could grind spices or touch different furs and fabrics. We had places to climb, including a wooden boat where we could pretend to be pirates and a structure made of ropes that challenged our balance. We also explored the preschool, imagining what children felt as they engaged with the environment. Our creativity was sparked and our imagination ignited. Bos and Leeman were inspirational.

During a playful conference, attendees are invited to challenge their own boundaries and experiment with risks, make mistakes, and find innovative alternative methods to learning—all through play. The idea is to disrupt the process of a traditional conference and try new approaches that increase their depth of practice, moving them from duplicating what they see to generating their own ideas. The concept of the depth of practice originated in the book *Design in Mind: A Framework for Sparking Ideas, Collaborations, and Innovation in Early Education* (Beloglovsky and Grant-Groves 2020). Educators can explore what they find difficult in exciting ways through playful engagement rather than repeating things they find easy.

Playfulness at the Center of Planning, Implementation, and Evaluation

From the planning of the conference through implementation and evaluation, the organizers' decisions need to be based on the following question: Do we dare just to play and have fun as we plan this conference?

Start by creating a sense of place and community. Consider the city that will host and the space selected for the meeting; these locations can help develop a sense of place and community. One of my most memorable conferences took place in Washington, DC. The events incorporated many historical monuments, and the buildings transported us in time and through a profound exploration, sparking conversations relevant to our work. For example, visiting museums dedicated to specific cultures or peoples can help us understand history and how it still influences the decisions we make today.

Let's translate the concept as we plan a conference that says: "Join us in play." In cities with a beach, participants can engage in a sandcastle competition, then talk about the properties of sand as a sensory experience after the contest to deepen learning. A town close to a forest allows people to explore the beauty of nature while imagining the play possibilities of outdoor ecosystems, segueing naturally into workshops about outdoor education. In an urban setting, hold part of the conference as an interactive visit to a children's museum or Exploratorium and offer workshops connected to tinkering and playing with unscripted materials as part of the visit. Do you get the idea? The city or town hosting the conference can have a lot to do with engaging a playful attitude and promoting learning, and the conference becomes an experience that creates memories that last for a long time.

Imagine that from the moment you enter the space (the beach, museum, historical building, and so on) to the moment you leave, the experience stimulates your senses and invites you to play and be joyful. The registration booth is interactive, and you are asked to complete several gamification challenges. Participants get points when exchanging virtual or real business cards with others. You may even encourage participants to create playful business cards with riddles and jokes. Everyone gets a tube of bubbles as a welcoming gift. Music is playing, and it is fun and playful. You see spontaneous dancing erupting. Art projected on the walls immerses you into colors, shapes, and moving landscapes. The conference catalog encourages people to use social media to post short videos sharing playful moments. Attendees with the most innovative videos can be highlighted throughout the conference and receive prizes.

Provide tables with Loose Parts and other unscripted tools and materials for people to play with and create transient collective art. Participants can share photos of their creations with others. Other joyful options could include the following:

- Set up open play areas throughout the conference. Big games such as giant Jenga blocks, Twister, Connect Four, and a ball pit engage attendees by taking them down memory lane while encouraging big-body movements.

- Encourage impromptu competitions that invite connection and networking by providing hula hoops and various balls with corresponding goals (such as basketballs with a basketball hoop).

- Large, double-sided acrylic easels and gigantic wooden puzzles are beautiful, interactive decor that help people network while they play.

Playrooms, Tinkering Labs, and Play Studios

Throughout the conference, make playrooms available that simulate play spaces in early childhood ecosystems but on a large scale. Invite exhibitors to sponsor playroom spaces and provide educational media, tools, and materials. Consider:

- Construction and building spaces invite attendees to play with blocks and natural Loose Parts. Provide a woodworking station with tools and a sanding table. Create a demonstration play lab (a designated space to test and prototype ideas) where attendees can explore and be fully engaged with a variety of tools and materials; for example, set up a light and shadow lab.

- Participants can use fabric and other props in an imagination space to dress up and engage in pretend play sequences. Also include areas with musical instruments for impromptu performances and perhaps a photo booth to record the moment. During the day, improv facilitators engage attendees in exploring techniques that they can use in the classroom. Musicians can stop by to discuss how music can be engaging and interactive. Dancers can invite people to explore movement.

- Attendees can explore different media and open exploration experiences in a visual arts space. For instance, this space can include Loose Parts to create an ongoing collective mural, materials for weaving a collective work of art, or a station to explore the properties of clay. An artist in residence can create invitations and guide attendees' exploration of the elements of arts and process art while also discussing how art can be integrated into early childhood ecosystems.

- Create a Loose Parts room with multiple items for attendees to tinker with, mess about, and enjoy a creative moment. Support conversation and convene reflective circles to discuss the language of the materials and how they support play and learning. Workshops on curating and infusing Loose Parts into ecosystems will invite attendees to test ideas.

- Curate a quiet space to read children's books or explore books educators may want to purchase. Have comfortable places to sit, and play relaxing background music to calm spirits. Schedule authors to read aloud and discuss their books.

Plan Playful Evenings to Renew and Reboot

The evenings are planned to continue the experience to connect us to our playful, creative, and innovative spirits.

JUST PLAY! CHALLENGE

- Set up improv group workshops so people can let go of expectations and give free rein to their playfulness. They can pretend to be a character or just be witty and playful.

- An evening with a musician brings people together. Or let loose and make new friends at karaoke night by singing to both children's songs and adult music.

- Create an atmosphere of wonder and engagement with lanterns and LED lights. The ambience invites people to connect with times when they gathered with family and had sing-alongs or told stories around the campfire or a fireplace.

- Host a magic workshop to teach simple tricks educators can use to inspire children's play. Magic invites us to wonder and try to figure out how a trick was done. It is an invitation to suspend what we know and explore the power of illusion.

- Spend time playing in the Loose Parts lab. Let your creativity expand as you play with unscripted materials.

Ask yourself: How would I feel attending a conference that invites me to play?

Adding an Element of Surprise

The element of surprise keeps attendees ready to see what happens next. This reminds me of the atmosphere created at the Magic Castle in Los Angeles. When you step into the castle, you never know what to expect. A strolling magician might demonstrate card tricks to visitors waiting in line for a show or dinner. A ghost might walk by. In other words, the venue keeps guests continually entertained. The same element of surprise can be incorporated into a conference:

- Build excitement by incorporating unexpected guests and presenters.

- Offer pop-up giveaways at unforeseen times.

- Create a new play space in the middle of the conference.

- Announce surprise evening events.

- Change a room from a typical conference hall setting to a more relaxed living room style.

The idea is to keep attendees guessing what will happen that day—and even that can become a guessing contest with prizes.

Playful Gatherings That Enhance Creativity and Innovation

Regardless of the conference theme, creativity and innovation should be the drivers so we are continually striving to bring sustainable change into education. An experience needs to begin with a human-centric perspective. Build empathy into the planning, implementation, and delivery of every aspect of the event. We know that many educators are feeling burnout and are ready to quit. More than ever, they need to be immersed in an experience that sparks their creative spirit. When I attend conferences, I notice that educators attend to learn and disconnect and perhaps party and celebrate. Understanding that they need regeneration can help event planners create an experience that will spark attendees' interest and hopefully lessen their burnout.

The conference experience must include opportunities to ideate, innovate, and creatively problem solve. For instance, set up a design lab where designers, architects, and engineers guide conversations and attendees can join ideation moments centered on general-interest challenges and questions guided by people who understand design thinking. This engages participants in the process of designing, prototyping, and implementing an idea. For instance, create an experience exploring the concepts of invitations and provocations and how they guide children's interests. Ideas that emerge from the design lab can be uploaded into an interactive virtual platform to receive feedback and then tested in tinker labs. Attendees can revisit their work to enhance it until they are ready to introduce it into their early childhood ecosystems. Imagine bringing home the best "takeaway" ever. You have not only an idea that has been prototyped and tested but also the knowledge of how you can apply design thinking to your ecosystem.

Designing Playful Workshops and Presentations

To continue to engage in learning through play, speakers' proposals should include a "just play" element and interactive component. Presentations are selected both for the content and playful delivery as well as their ability to facilitate active learning wherein participants learn by thinking, ideating, designing, investigating, and creating.

As part of the proposal, the presenters can create an avatar of the audience they are presenting to. The avatar has a name and a clear identity. To make it more fun and meaningful, they can add a photo or a sketch of their avatar. They can consider the following questions:

- Who is the avatar that will benefit from the presentation?
- What are its cultural values (identity, history, tradition, language, values)?
- What are its dreams, desires, and expectations?
- Where does it live (geographical location, place, and community)?
- What are its strengths, knowledge, and skills?
- What will the avatar's day look like?
- What challenges does it experience?
- What joyful moments does it have?

Add all the workshop avatars to a display wall at the conference. Attendees can also add to the avatar wall to show others who they are as a professional.

Presentations need to keep the audience engaged, playing with words, with ideas, with new perspectives. Play explorations increase enthusiasm and generate ideas. For instance, if you introduce a topic and invite participants to play and represent their understanding of the topic, it will help you identify gaps and provide any needed support. Focus on a question-driven approach that engages curiosity. It can be a problem to solve or mystery to explore. An informal process makes people more open to sharing ideas, bestows confidence, and inspires commitment to exploring a situation jointly. For example, when people can represent their community by using Loose Parts, they are more open to play and share their ideas.

Extend the impact and reach of a presentation by designing an artifact participants can take with them and easily implement when they get back to work. Recently I talked to a colleague who painted a rock at a workshop and placed it in her office as a reminder to be creative and play.

The keynote presentation needs to motivate and inspire people to engage in daily play and cultivate a playful attitude, to be present and experience awe, wonder, and delight. Play must be central to the keynote to unlock participants' creativity, joy, connectedness, and innovative thinking. It must open our thinking to endless possibilities and increase curiosity. It should help us connect to one another and create a sense of belonging to something that is greater than ourselves.

Networking with Play

One of the most challenging yet essential parts of attending a conference is networking. I remember attending conferences and dreading introducing myself to people. I also felt stressed out when I saw people planning to go out at night, myself excluded. It felt like I was back in school, the last person selected to play a sport or a game. Play makes networking less stressful and more engaging.

Creating intentional networking opportunities is an integral part of planning a conference. Begin by removing hierarchy so people can connect without worrying they are not at the same level. Labels like "Speaker" on the name tag or other ribbons that denote jobs, honors, and recognition can be barriers to true connection. I have to admit, I am not much for using name tags. I think they interfere with an honest, "Hi, how are you, my name is . . ." Name tags also make me self-conscious because they usually land on your chest and people have to stare there. If you must have name tags, give attendees the opportunity to create the ribbons they want to include on their name tag, with more meaningful labels than mere job titles. Ask them to come up with words that describe how they dare to play.

● PLAYFUL TRANSFORMATION CHALLENGE ●

Invite attendees to create play groups when they register, and have them start messaging one another. That way, when they get to the conference, they have already communicated with other attendees and have an automatic connection. Several years ago, there was a trending game that had people chasing Pokémon figures and collecting tokens that could help them gain higher levels. It was a fun way to be active. I have to say, even I got into it for a few weeks. Imagine a similar game at a conference, where people look for others who are wearing a button with a QR code. When the code is scanned, a character is revealed with part of a quote related to the conference theme. The idea is to collect all the parts of the quote to win points that can lead to a bigger prize at the end of the conference. Many quotes can be circulated to make the game more exciting. Participants can be asked if they are willing to wear a button when they register. The quotes are shared in a conference app that tabulates the people who complete the quotes. The QR codes get harder to find as the conference progresses, so there are only a few winners who find a complete quote. Keep a level of simplexity (complex, yet simple) to ensure that conference attendees are engaged and do not give up.

Create a similar interactive game by having a few volunteers wear a distinctive scarf or hat. When participants spot the people wearing the scarf or hat, they take a picture at the location and challenge other participants to find the person with the scarf and hat. The photos are posted on the app. At the end of the conference, the person who takes the most pictures in different locations wins a prize.

Addressing Questions and Barriers

I will pause a moment here to address some of the questions that are probably percolating in your mind. These are likely the same questions that I am asking myself. Take time to write down the questions and doubts you have. Be authentic. After you write the questions, decide the motivation behind your question, with honesty.

● Can the theme of the conference change while we maintain a playful attitude?

I will venture to say yes. Some topics may seem more serious than playful and command a more scholarly approach. However, a captivating experience can still be created. For example, if the conference's theme is linked to creating equitable and inclusive education, then anti-bias work, racism, oppression, and privilege will be addressed. These are not playful concepts and will require a different experience. The focus of the experience can be on creating a sense of community and connecting people who can work together to make a change. Change and advocacy still require playful leaders who use humor to connect. Storytellers can be part of the experience, and the music can represent multicultural and historical genres. The improv troupe can focus on techniques used in Theatre of the Oppressed, created by Brazilian playwright Augusto Boal, to uncover injustice and bias. Each of the spaces described here can incorporate invitations to explore cultural values, history, language, and traditions.

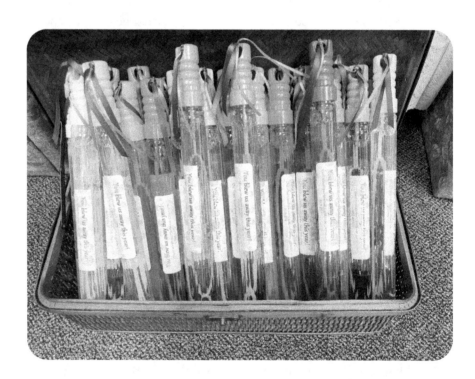

- Can this type of experience be affordable?

  When I worked in the entertainment industry, one of my responsibilities was the production of conferences and exhibits. We did have a large budget, but we also had to negotiate and conserve resources. The key is collaboration. Instead of one association or company assuming full responsibility, gather people, businesses, agencies, and community organizers to leverage resources and work together. To create an experience requires a shift in mindset. Creativity and playfulness become the driving force, and the cost can be leveraged and managed.

- Will people receive the experience authentically?

  Are we presenting the experience with enough authenticity to engage participants' interest and ideas? Can we stretch their thinking by offering challenges and complexity? If the answer to these questions is yes, you'll get the best wholehearted participation possible. If the answer is no, reflect on what changes you could make so that the experience authentically elicits playfulness.

Reflections

- Next time you attend or plan a conference, what playful opportunities will you create for yourself or others?

- How will you approach networking using a more playful approach?

- What strategies will you incorporate in the planning of a conference to make it more playful and engaging?

- Next time you present at a conference, what play opportunities will you include In your presentation?

CHAPTER 8

The Adult Place in the Early Childhood Ecosystem

Play is distinct from "ordinary" life both as to locality and duration. This is the third main characteristic of play: its secludedness, its limitedness. It is "played out" within certain limits of time and place. It contains its own course and meaning.

—Johan Huizinga

When I graduated with a bachelor's degree in radio, television, and film, I worked in the entertainment industry for a few years. One of the companies I worked for made every effort to create a sense of playfulness that kept me excited every day. Don't get me wrong, it was hard work and a competitive environment. However, humor and anticipating what surprises would happen next kept us engaged and joyful. There were surprise lunches, monthly breakfasts with raffles, private screenings for new movies and shows, invitations to premiers and parties, days at the races, and many other events. Almost every day would see something surprising happening. When I stepped off the elevator and headed to my office, I would encounter colleagues laughing and planning to surprise one another. The physical space looked like just another corporate space, but the atmosphere was both glamorous and fun.

What created the playful atmosphere was the rhythm of the day, feeling the anticipation that we would frequently get to experience something new. We worked together and laughed together, and there was a sense of camaraderie. Playfulness can create patterns and rhythms in both the physical and social space that bring joy to the work space.

We now realize that play and playfulness are a crucial part of life. Play is an intrinsic, healthy human drive, and it is how we maneuver the complexities and stresses of the environment. When we are playful, we get stronger physically, emotionally, socially, creatively, and spiritually. We must design an ecosystem that promotes play for children and adults alike. To bring playfulness into the early childhood ecosystem, we must remember that everyone who shares the space has different perspectives and play archetypes that need to be incorporated into the daily experiences.

Educators spend over eight hours a day in the early childhood ecosystem. They share the space with children, families, and colleagues. Educators work as neuronal architects, interior designers, listeners, curricula developers, holders of emotions, mediators, and much more. Yet many early childhood ecosystems are designed to teach academics or specific topics. The walls are covered in colorful bulletin boards that seldom represent the reality of the people living in the space. Recently many early childhood programs have embraced creating aesthetically pleasing spaces. These spaces often look like a photo shoot for *Architectural Digest* magazine rather than spaces for living and learning as a community. But what we should really be doing is creating ecosystems that authentically represent the people who inhabit the space: places where children and adults see themselves represented, where playfulness guides the practices, and where joyfulness is promoted with respect and responsiveness to play and culture.

In early childhood spaces, the focus is often on children, and the adult is left out of the planning. I often joke that educators in low child chairs have to sit in the grasshopper pose. Their legs are up to their ears. Their bodies are hurting at the end of the day, and movement is slower, which means it is harder to feel playful or engage in meaningful interactions. It is essential to remember that adults also inhabit the early childhood ecosystem, and we must hold space for them. We all experience autonomy and growth through play. Because play is the catalyst for joy, it requires spaces that also integrate the adults' perspective. It is time we revisit how we design early childhood ecosystems to include the adults who also share the space.

Designing a Playful Space

I begin the conversation with a question. What does a playful space look like? To make ecosystems more playful, we must consider the following essential elements:

- The ecosystem is anchored in the authentic lives of the people who inhabit it, so we must begin by defining all the people who live and learn there.

- Playfulness is seen in every aspect of the ecosystem as adults and children play, create, laugh, and share the space.

- The prevailing message is one of belonging, respect, joy, and trust.

Holding space to encourage playfulness involves redesigning our physical, temporal, and socio-emotional spaces. A seamless flow of patterns and rhythms in a playful ecosystem creates inclusion and equity. Our beautiful planet also has rhythms that move smoothly from day to night. The seasons change, and they easily flow into each other. The sun moves across the sky, the moon waxes and wanes through its phases, and the stars embellish our evenings. The geography of our space and the places where we live influence our lives. The same is true for our workplaces.

In most early childhood ecosystems, the rhythm and patterns of the day are established by interactions. When the interactions are joyful, children and adults discover more pleasure and explore and learn together. When adults are playful, they are more willing and capable of designing play spaces that are inviting and engaging.

When we embrace the idea that playfulness is the predisposition to reframe situations with humor and authentic positivity, it leads us to create ecosystems that encourage innovation. In a playful ecosystem, adults generate new ideas, grow in their learning, and regenerate their depth of practice. The ecosystem design represents the understanding that play is essential—play from the scientific, biological, and developmental understanding and not from an adult-invented (mythical) perspective. In other words, the adults engaged in designing the play spaces must have profound knowledge and experience of what play means because they have played themselves. Play spaces must allow us as adults to take risks, test boundaries, and reflect on our perceptions and understanding of children. Educators who design for play must be humble and accept that they are tourists in the children's spaces and that they have to be welcomed in.

Any play space we design needs to include opportunities to perform, dance, tell stories, and verbalize ideas. The space needs to imagine what is possible and perhaps what may not seem likely. Spaces must allow us to be magicians and enter into worlds created by our imaginations. Most important, the places we design must ensure that the process is joyful and engaging.

The Welcoming Space

Let's begin with the first place adults see as they enter the ecosystem. What are the messages conveyed by the entrance? Does it say, "The person in the office and behind the high desk is the person in power"? Or does it say, "Everyone is welcome here, and we have created spaces where you can sit, join in the play, and have a conversation?" In a welcoming space, there is ample light, and the space is open for exploration. People can take their time to discover the sensory experiences on the walls and pathways. Plants, flowers, and natural materials are incorporated throughout the ecosystem. The art and photographs on the walls represent the current community enriching the ecosystem, including photos of children and adults laughing and playing together. As educators walk through the space, they encounter more representations of play experiences. There are small worlds (miniature playscapes that invite dramatic play, such as fairy spaces, forests with animal figures, and so on), whimsical art, and documentation from the children and adults who live in the ecosystem.

The Lounge

In the staff lounge, educators see comfortable chairs, games, and Loose Parts inviting them to play. (I prefer the term *lounge* to the terms *staff work space* or *office*.) Natural elements and light are an integral part of the space design. Staff take turns creating the mystery game of the week, wherein everyone works together to solve real challenges or made-up stories designed just for fun. You can hear laughter and joy. Coffee, tea, water, and healthy snacks are available. Everyone is represented in playful photographs and quotes that inspire play. The lounge feels like home, and it releases the daily stressors of being an educator. Soft music plays, and educators take turns choosing what they want to listen to. A fountain occupies a space on one of the walls, and the peaceful sound is calming and centering. The lounge is a place to replenish your energy and take a break from work tasks. Its message is, "You are here to breathe, relax, meditate, and play."

The Inner Yard and Hallways

As people walk to the classrooms, they cross through spaces filled with opportunities to explore creativity. Small and large wall easels allow adults and children to paint side by side. A wall with Plexiglas invites us to draw our collective ideas and thoughts. If the building has a courtyard or other large open space, it features natural enclosures where adults and children can sit together to read and quietly talk. Swing benches and sitting hammocks invite chilling throughout the day. A sound garden produces music and invites adults and children to play with the instruments, wind chimes, and various Loose Parts. Once again, the message is "Join us to play and be joyful together." Consider the available space as you make the invitations to play accessible and flexible.

The Classroom

When we walk into the classroom ecosystem, the first thing we hear is children and adults laughing together. There is an ongoing flow of play both outdoors and indoors. Space design is human centered to create harmony, with comfortable sofas and chairs of different sizes for adults and children to sit and gather. The walls incorporate children's art, for example, featuring children's framed work arranged in an aesthetic composition. Clutter on the walls is kept to a minimum, and wall displays highlight what is truly representative of the community. There is harmony in the space's textures, colors, materials, and sounds. The message is "Come and play and be your authentic self."

The Temporal Space

An ecosystem designed for play requires dedicated time; adults must be given time to play and explore throughout the day. There must also be times to engage in reflection, to help educators make connections to the power of play and understand how children grow and learn when adults have a playful attitude.

Imagine a Playful Place: The Play Studio

One idea for creating a culture of playfulness that really inspires me is the adult play studio. I envision these spaces to be separate from the current workrooms, which are meant to store materials and support the work in the classroom. The studio is a place to play, innovate, and try out ideas that emerge both individually and collectively. In other words, it is an adult play space.

Imagine a place where you can do the following:

- Freely play with your ideas.

- Test your theories.

- Develop techniques and inspirations to keep you playing and exploring with confidence.

- Envision an abundance of play possibilities.

- Make mistakes and conquer your fears.

- Gather with a friend to reflect, plan, and design together.

- Approach your work with a playful way of knowing and being.

- Just wonder.

A play studio for adults to tinker, mess about, and experiment provides opportunities for growth as educators and human beings. In the studio, we can revisit our childhood memories and dream of new possibilities. The studio opens the opportunity to build relationships with people, the space, and the materials. In the play studio, we can play, take risks, and be daring. The play studio is designed to engage adults in play, expand their curiosity, and encourage them to wonder what can happen right now and in the future. More important, in the play studio we can connect with the joy of childhood because we are allowed to be ourselves. Perhaps if we start to see the world, feel the world, and explore the world through the eyes, hearts, and hands of children, we can then create genuine opportunities for them to play, be creative, and be joyful.

Ideally, educators develop several studios to explore different play concepts or rotate the explorations throughout the year. The rhythm of the interactions will guide educators' decisions on when to transition the space to a different exploration.

Hold playful reflective circles for educators to explore their learning and ideas and consider how their own play informs the way they create play opportunities for young children. Embrace the process. Be creative and bold. The only limitation comes from our fear of change and the unknown. Imagine what it would be like to be curious about the unknown instead. Ask, "What will I learn? How will I grow? What experiences will I have? What thoughts and ideas will emerge? How will the unknown journey connect me to the children, families, and colleagues?" I don't know about you, but when I ask all these questions, I get excited. I don't necessarily want answers. Instead, I just want to continue to play, experiment, and go with the flow so that I can give full rein to my creativity.

The following ideas show how the studio can be designed and changed as your own play evolves.

The Light and Shadows Play Studio

The space is designed for exploring light and shadows fully. There are light tables, overhead projectors, and LED lights on the floor, the walls, and the ceiling. The windows let in light throughout the day, so educators can explore their differences. There are also black lights and fluorescent items to deepen the investigation. Flowy and transparent fabrics suspended from the ceiling dance and move in light and in shadows and show the concepts of transparency and opacity. Mirrors add depth and three-dimensionality. Loose Parts and various art media are available so that educators can represent their explorations.

The light and dark studio can easily transition to an exploration of art and design. Use light to explore colors—black, white, and different shades of gray. Educators can use the light tables to examine the transparency and opacity of objects and how they affect color perception. Playing with color gives us a deeper understanding of how color influences our thoughts, feelings, and perceptions. One of my favorite explorations is mixing paint to create different shades and hues. I start with the primary colors and tabulate how many colors I can make. I then add black and white paint and experiment with the effects of mixing them with each color. The process is playful and relaxing. Each color elicits a reaction that can be anything from jubilant to underwhelmed when the color is not what was expected. Mixing colors allows for mistakes (which are really learning opportunities), and it engages our senses.

The Art and Design Studio

To continue playing with art and design, incorporate different media. For example, try playing with types of charcoal: vine, willow, nitram, powdered charcoal, compressed charcoal, and charcoal pencil. Also try pastel, Conté, graphite, and natural charcoal, used mainly for barbecue grills (the type not infused with lighter fluid, of course). Explore charcoals on different types of paper and surfaces. How hard or how soft the charcoal is makes a difference in how it supports drawing. Remember that the idea is to play and experiment with the materials and not test our drawing abilities.

I love the movement and transformation of watercolor paints when liquid is added or subtracted. Watercolors come in tubes, pans, liquid, pencils, markers, sheets, pastels, and sticks. Exploring different types of paper and tools can add texture and enhance the play. Combine bubbles with liquid watercolor or use straws to blow and move the liquid around. Layer different types of watercolor to better understand the properties of the materials.

The Loose Parts Studio

Explore ephemeral art and design with Loose Parts and natural materials. Spending time just playing, creating, constructing, and deconstructing with Loose Parts deepens our knowledge about the importance of play in increasing creativity and innovation. Ephemeral art first appeared in the 1960s as artists took their art outside the walls of a museum or art gallery, stepping away from selling art for profit. Instead, their focus was on the process of playing with the materials. Ephemeral art engages the artist or player to construct and deconstruct at will. There is no expectation for a final product. There are no constraints or expectations as to when the process is completed, and it immerses us in accepting change and everything unknown or unpredictable. Like play, ephemeral art is owned by the person creating the work. The interaction between the person and the materials guides the process and actions. Another beautiful part of ephemeral art is that it teaches us not to value materialism. Not everything we create has to be displayed. The process of creation is fulfilling enough. Ephemeral art teaches us about the impermanence of life and nature and increases our appreciation for living in the moment. After all, the seasons come and go, and each gives us different gifts. Sunrises and sunsets are never permanent. Ephemeral art is a moment in time made briefly tangible.

The Construction Studio

Playing with construction materials such as blocks, ramps, tubes, and so on can be exciting as we learn how materials can be combined and represent our perspectives on the world around us. Constructing and deconstructing helps us understand the properties of the materials. The affordances of the blocks become apparent as we touch them and act on them. There are now so many different types of blocks: Dr. Drew's Discovery Blocks, Kapla blocks, unit blocks, magnetic blocks, acrylic blocks, and so much more. Just the idea of having a room filled with blocks is a powerful invitation to play.

The Nature Studio

A nature play studio entices us to explore natural materials indoors. Different types of sand in containers invite us to create Zen gardens. Each sand is different, and the texture varies from smooth to grainy. The colors are magnificent, from deep red to almost white. I love getting my hands into Jurassic sand. Combining the sand with driftwood and shells or adding small rakes and other tools for mark-making helps us connect to the ephemeral properties of nature. I have a particular love for stones and can spend hours exploring and analyzing them, balancing, stacking, and combining them to create cairns, sculptures, and art. Whenever I go to a lapidary store, I make sure to feel the surface of as many gemstones as possible. Driftwood likewise features intriguing textures and formations. Balancing pieces and laying them in intricate patterns can inspire us to sustain our environment. So many possibilities.

The Clay Studio

Set up a clay studio where people can explore the properties of different types of clay: earthenware clay, stoneware clay, ball clay, porcelain, and so on. Each type feels and behaves differently. What clays do have in common is how they stimulate our senses. Make space in the play studio to roll, flatten, and sculpt the clay, learning about its plasticity and molding or modeling capacities. Use simple and complex tools. If possible, add a pottery wheel. There is a freeing sensation in the moment we place our wet hands on the slowly spinning wheel. Clay invites us to poke, pinch, twist, and roll. There is something pleasurable about realizing the effect our actions have on the clay and how it responds to the ways we manipulate it. Play with clay is an invitation to get dirty and messy without fears or constraints.

Playful Considerations

It is essential to remember that the studio is a place we can trust—a place without judgment or criticism. The purpose is to have a place where we can fully immerse ourselves in play and explore our capacities to innovate. In the studio, we can join as a community of educators to play, reflect, and dream together. We know that unscripted play holds the space for creativity, and the more we play as adults, the more we will give children the same opportunities to play. When we can go beyond what we believe we are allowed to do, we grow as educators. We learn to trust ourselves and our intuition. We know that mistakes are opportunities for growth and that the disequilibrium that emerges in play is the beginning of learning. A play studio allows us to be vulnerable and embrace the mystery of the unknown. As we play, we allow ourselves to make room for uncertainty and have the courage to do new things with confidence and authenticity. Play reawakens our senses of curiosity and awe.

When play is infused into any ecosystem, we plan to ensure that the play or game is the following:

- Easy to understand
- Easy to play
- Easy to quit
- Safe

- Fun
- Inclusive and equitable
- Voluntary
- Nonthreatening

Don't look for final answers or outcomes. Instead, be playful.

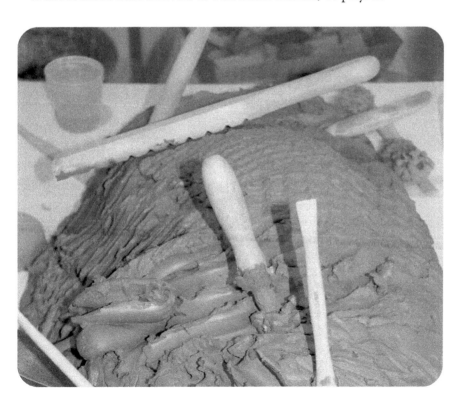

JUST PLAY! CHALLENGE

Every morning, post a play challenge on the board. The following are some ideas.

● How many ways can you turn a negative into a positive experience? You can start with something as simple as, "I had pizza for dinner last night, and it was not so good." Someone may write in response, "But you still ate it because any pizza is better than no pizza!" The idea is to see who comes up with the funniest line.

● Invite people to write down the many ways they are playful. Ask one day for ways they are playful at work, another day for ways they are playful at home. Or ask what object makes you playful or what person and so on.

● Invite educators to share a play memory from childhood by writing it on a sticky note and attaching it to a whiteboard. The game can be extended by placing the sticky notes in a container. Each week an educator picks a memory and re-creates it for the rest of the staff to explore. Encourage the educators to recall unscripted play memories to bring more true play into the exploration.

● Add a simple provocation in the form of a question:

  • What idea do you have today?

  • What design do you have in mind?

  • What theory do you want to test or explore today?

● Bring in a new book and invite people to write or draw a simple review. Educators can take turns bringing in a book too. This is a great way to play with words and images while getting helpful feedback in curating the books we add to the ecosystem.

Keep it playful with a variety of games:

- Mystery play: Solve a crime. Leave clues and puzzles throughout the week that will lead to solving the mystery. The twist is that the more people collaborate, the faster they will find the answer. You can create your own game to represent people in the program, or you can purchase a commercial mystery game.

- Play an ongoing collective game of Scrabble. The purpose is not to see who will win but instead see how many words can be created with the tiles. You can make it more complex by adding braille or ASL tiles.

- Wrap the furniture, the floor, and the walls in the lounge in Bubble Wrap. I find that popping Bubble Wrap is joyful and relaxing.

- Place a large canvas with tempera paint, brushes, and perhaps other media for educators to express their ideas in art. Better yet, cover the floor and the walls with butcher paper for educators to paint. For me, it satisfies the urge we had to paint the walls when we first discovered crayons and markers as children.

- Bring games from around the world for educators to explore. Research ahead of time games that are representative of the diverse community of people who live and learn in the ecosystem.

- Bring a large set of Jenga blocks. It can be left in the lounge to entice collaboration and engagement. Everyone can join at different times.

- Gradually build the biggest rubber band ball or foil ball you can.

Ask yourself: How do I feel walking into a place where play is valued? How will I re-create the playfulness in my work with children?

Remind one another that the purpose of play is to keep you playful. Being playful means that you are present and in the moment. Playfulness also makes us responsive, attentive, and creative. Playfulness makes us let go of constraints and become part of something larger than ourselves. That is why all of the adults who live, play, and learn in the ecosystem have the responsibility to contribute to creating a culture of playfulness.

Reflections

- How is the adult represented in your space?

- What will you do to make the space more playful for both adults and children?

- How will you use the outdoor space to offer adult playtime?

- What is the welcome message adults receive as they walk into the space?

CHAPTER 9

Designing Outdoor Spaces That Encourage Playfulness

Play is a constant happening, a constant
act of creation in the mind or in practise.

—Arvid Bengtsson

Our outdoor spaces help us refocus our energy and encourage children
and adults to share their collective imagination, ideas, and interests. When
I imagine spaces that bring joy, the first thing that comes to mind is bonding. Outdoor spaces are healing, relaxing, restorative, and invigorating.
We reclaim our energy and anchor ourselves to the earth's rhythm when
we are outdoors. A well-designed and provisioned outdoor space helps us
find harmony. Outdoor ecosystems where adults can play and wonder help
them value play in children. To create a culture of playfulness, we must

design spaces that are inviting and build anticipation. When adults feel creative and playful, they likely transmit the same emotions. Many of the spaces described next encourage play in both adults and children.

A thoughtfully designed playscape focusing on nature is an alternative to traditional playgrounds. Playscapes are directly connected to the local environment and geography. The following are some principles of playscapes that invite adults and children to play:

- Natural playscapes offer multisensory, genuine experiences. Nature is the focus and guides the play.

- Every outdoor space element is unscripted and designed to encourage divergent uses.

- The Loose Parts encourage experimentation. They are meant to be touched, moved, combined, dug up, built, or engaged in open exploration.

- Plants are selected to represent the native landscape and to stimulate the senses.

- The environment promotes risk-taking and collaborative, active, and individual play.

The following are some features for outdoor playscapes to consider.

Gardens and Edible Landscapes

There is something fulfilling about gardening, getting down on our knees and using our hands to move dirt, make holes, and pull weeds—and then finally eating the plants we have grown. It also helps adults connect with children's curiosity about dirt, worms, and bugs. Gardening is a playful way to understand the rhythm of nature and your geographical location. From harvesting delicate leafy greens in early spring to pumpkins in the fall and hearty kale and cabbage in the winter, collecting the bounty of our efforts adds health and joy to our life. Keep it simple with raised beds or container gardens. Planting in pots makes it easy to bring plants indoors if the weather isn't cooperating and can extend the life of an herb garden. The smell of herbs, both outdoors and indoors, can be invigorating. Educators can add playfulness to the garden by creating small worlds with fairies or other surprising and delightful creatures.

Organize a day when all the adults in the program meet in the garden and just play with dirt. Turn the soil over, get it wet, and make mud. Feel the texture and smell its earthy freshness. Perhaps acclimate to that inevitable worm or bug you might usually avoid touching. Playing in the dirt allows you to make mistakes, encounter fears, and become connected with the earth. Turning over dirt buckets and moving the dirt with shovels and rakes can be calming. Playing with dirt reminds many people of their childhoods. The child in me still remembers jumping in piles of fresh dirt or digging in the garden with my grandfather.

Play with small worlds. I have fond memories of creating miniature imaginary worlds when I was a child. My favorite was fairy gardens. I think adults enjoy playing with small worlds as much as children do. Just walk through a plant nursery; most have a wide selection of miniature furniture, creatures, and other items to create small worlds in containers. Place them in different areas of the outdoor ecosystem, alongside baskets with Loose Parts and miniatures. Invite educators and families to create small worlds, and then walk around and play in one another's miniature spaces. After enough time has passed, sit down together and debrief the experience.

Ask yourself: How did it feel to engage in imaginary play? What else could I add to the small worlds? How will children be invited and engaged in small world play?

Water, Puddles, Water Walls, Streams, and Fountains

Nothing is more restorative than the sight and sound of water. It reduces stress and makes us happy. My mother always reminded me to look at the water because it was healing. When I am stressed, I go outside and water the plants and listen to the sound of the water as it falls and puddles. I also love being by the ocean, a river, or a lake and getting my feet wet as I watch the rippling movement of the water. Water features create a feeling of calm and stimulate the senses of touch, sight, and hearing.

Adults love to play with water as much as children do. I have memories of running through the sprinklers with my children and enjoying it as much as they did. When my oldest turned four years old, the temperature in Los Angeles reached 110, and we had to rethink her birthday party. I got spray bottles, filled balloons with water, and had small pools around the yard for children to stay cool. I did not expect the adults to have as much fun playing as the children, yet we were silly and playful and joined in the water play without distracting the children. I found myself filling more water balloons and spray bottles. Luckily, I had purchased a lot of both.

It is such a pleasure to jump into a puddle after it has rained. I was born in Guadalajara, Mexico, and I have fond memories of walking around the neighborhood when it was raining. As it became soaked by rain, the scent of the earth always reminded me of the clay used by a local ceramic artist. It was fresh and wonderful. Puddles are open invitations to play. In your outdoor space, experiment with arranging large river rocks to capture water that the earth can later absorb. It is a sustainable and engaging way to inspire playfulness, and it can even entice adults to jump in the puddles and relive childhood memories.

In Roseville Community Preschool, Bev Bos and Michael Leeman designed a self-sustaining lentic ecosystem. Lentic ecosystems include standing water such as ponds, marshes, lakes, and swamps. Creating this type of ecosystem is another form of intellectual and engaging play. It begins with research, learning about the components, containers, and types of plants that will work best. Once the investigation (part of the fun!) is completed, the actual design and building phases begin. At this stage, physical play is central. Touching the plants, sand, gravel, moss, and maybe small water animals connects us to the rhythm of an ecosystem and revives our playful attitude. The finished ecosystem is beautiful and requires very little upkeep, and watching it grow brings interest and playfulness into the environment.

Creative and ever-changing water walls showcase the movement of water to engage people in play. The water reflecting the sun creates fascinating optical illusions as adults and children pour water into the wall. Create a water wall using recyclable items: attach tubes and funnels to wooden pallets (propped up or hung vertically on a wall), and place a large container at the bottom to capture the water for reuse. To make the water wall more complex, hang the tubes so they can be moved into different configurations.

Plan a day for water play—it is guaranteed to elicit laughter and promote joy! To keep hydrated, have drinks and fruit popsicles (*paletas*, as we call them in Mexico) available to enjoy throughout the day.

A side note: Some of the play ideas listed here can be easily adapted to do with children. However, the purpose of the following suggestions is not teaching you new things to do as an educator but rather an invitation to just play. Making this distinction at the beginning of the day is crucial for successful engagement.

Sponge Toss. Divide into several teams of no more than five people, and give each team a dry bucket with a minimum of ten sponges per team member. Also provide water-filled buckets, one per team, and line them up at one end of the yard. Ask teams to line up at a throwing distance in front of the buckets. The game starts as each player tries to toss their dry sponges into their team's water bucket. Once all of a team's sponges hit the target, the team retrieves its bucket, moves it to the opposite end of the yard, and starts throwing the wet sponges into the empty dry bucket. The team that gets all of its wet sponges into the bucket first wins. Dry sponges are harder to throw because they do not have much weight, so the sooner they get soaked, the faster the game moves. You can also change the rules and create new opportunities. For example, teams can retrieve the sponges and dunk them in water to toss them again.

Pass the Water Cup. Players make two equal single-file lines, with everyone facing forward. The first person fills a cup from a water bucket and passes it to the person behind them without turning to look at them. The second person passes to the third person, and so on. The team that gets the cup to the end of the line while spilling the least amount of water wins. To add complexity, make tiny holes in the bottom of the cups without telling people. This makes it harder to keep the water in the cups, so they have to work faster.

Water Balloon Toss. For this game, pair up as partners. Each pair tosses a water balloon back and forth. Every time a player catches the water balloon, they take a step back. The last pair with an unbroken water balloon wins.

Spray Bottle Chase. The idea is to get everyone wet. No winners. No losers. Just play!

Spray Bottle Painting. Hang large white sheets or painter's canvas. Give players spray bottles filled with liquid watercolor and invite them to create a colorful mural.

Painting with Ice Cubes. Prepare in advance by filling an ice cube tray with liquid watercolors or tempera paint and inserting craft sticks as the liquid solidifies. Once frozen, use the cubes to paint. Watch how the paint transfers into the paper as it melts. For a variation, omit the craft sticks and skate the ice cubes around in wide, shallow boxes. This works as a solo activity or in groups.

Water Balloon Pendulums. Hang a string across the yard. Suspend water balloons from the line. Players pair up and use Ping-Pong or badminton rackets to hit the balloons and try to get each other wet.

Water Balloon Catapults. Make giant catapults using Loose Parts, such as wood planks, elastic bands, and natural materials. See who can propel the water balloons the farthest without breaking them. This game requires skill and intentionality as people plan how to build an effective catapult. They have to calculate the weight of the balloons, how far the balloons need to be propelled, and how much speed is okay before the balloons break.

Painting with Water. Dip paintbrushes into buckets filled with water, and "paint" the floor or the walls. Focus participants on the pleasure of creating process art without expecting a particular outcome.

Toilet Plunger Water Balloon Toss and Catch. Use toilet plungers (clean, of course) to toss and catch water balloons. This can be done in pairs or in a circle.

Use your creativity and imagination to plan the day. Remember, the planning process can be just as much fun!

Ask yourself: How did my creativity increase after playing with wet art media?

Pathways and Terrain

Incorporating playful elements along pathways increases engagement and invites us to explore using our bodies. Opportunities to jump, skip, balance on fallen tree branches, or climb up small hills bring excitement to any space. Adding a sensory pathway engages our playful side while stimulating us and helping us burn energy. Sensory pathways can also give our brain a break from the pressures of everyday activities.

Have you noticed how you use your body as you walk on different terrain? It is almost as if we engage in an orchestrated dance sequence that shifts from a gentler rhythm to a crescendo. For example, walking on sand requires us to work our leg muscles, yet it is soothing. And the experience shifts when we cross from dry to wet sand and back. When we walk on gravel, we need to balance our entire body while focusing our attention on our feet. When we climb or jump from stump to stump or across a suspended bridge, we reach a crescendo that requires our senses, brain, emotions, and physical capacities to come together to meet the challenge.

Imagine walking down a pathway surrounded by fragrant plants (rosemary, mint, and so on). Your feet encounter different sensory terrain: logs, rocks, sand, and gravel. You then see a bench for resting and daydreaming. Nearby you find a basket with books and Loose Parts. As you continue walking, you come to an open space where other adults and children are playing. You continue on another pathway and discover a water wall where children are watching blue water go through transparent tubing. Soon you cross a bridge, and at the other end, you find a large sandpit with Loose Parts, shovels, and buckets. The water hose is running at one end, creating a wet area that children and adults wielding plastic creatures are pretending is a jungle or a swamp.

When designing outdoor play spaces that invite adults in, it is vital to incorporate as many childhood memories as possible. Do you remember playing an imaginary game where you were jinxed if you touched a certain color of tile or stepped on a line or crack in the concrete? The same idea can be integrated into the pathways. Games such as hopscotch or nature tic-tac-toe can also motivate adults to play.

Encourage educators and families to explore the pathway barefoot. Invite them to feel the different textures with their feet and hands.

Ask educators to pair up and take turns guiding each other to explore the pathways blindfolded. Ask them to reflect on what they feel, learn, and experience as they touch and walk on the different surfaces.

Organize a day in nature. Visit a botanical garden, forest, lake, wetland, or any outdoor space nearby. Invite educators to engage in a photographic safari, taking close-ups and distance photographs to discover elements they had not noticed before. Remind them to be playful in their discoveries and also to put the camera down just to be present and enjoy the space. Select some of the photos taken and reflect on what each photo tells you about the experience.

Ask yourself: How can I incorporate more time outdoors and in contact with nature?

Hiding Places and Tunnels

One common childhood memory that many of us share is playing hide-and-seek. As a child, I loved the thrill of hiding. I remember the anticipation I felt as the person seeking started counting as we hid. I always wanted to find the most secluded and clever place to hide so they would not find me. But at the same time, I always hoped they would find me because I did not want to get lost.

Well-positioned hiding places offer a respite from the noise and activity of the day; they also add a sense of mystery and anticipation to the ecosystem. Large crates can become resting places—add a transparent curtain to make an imaginary hiding space. Tunnels made with tubes large enough to crawl into are inviting for both adults and children. Mazes created by planting shrubs and plants add excitement and playfulness to a space. Small wooden playhouses work for hiding or imaginary play.

● JUST PLAY! CHALLENGE ●

Designing
Outdoor Spaces
That Encourage
Playfulness

●

153

Gather in teams or pairs and go on a treasure hunt to find as many hiding places in the outdoor environment as possible.

Start an evening meeting or gathering with a game of hide-and-seek in the outdoor space. Illuminate the space with candelabras and lanterns. For a touch of color, incorporate glow sticks and bubbles. Fairy lights in the trees and shrubs add a sense of wonderment and playful fun. The game gives educators a creative way to analyze their outdoor environment while they are playing.

Use flashlights to create shadows and infuse mystery or to play tag. The "it" person can tag the others by pointing the flashlight at them.

Pop-Up Playgrounds

Invite educators to gather materials and create a pop-up adventure playground that celebrates child-directed play while also inviting adults in. Stock the space with Loose Parts (cardboard boxes, logs, tubes, crates, wood planks, and other natural materials) that can be moved and changed as the play evolves. The more we add movable and large Loose Parts to an area, the more the players take charge of the play. Pop-up adventure playgrounds provide opportunities for safe risk-taking and freedom. They also welcome people of all ages and abilities to play together and explore without facing judgment. Teams can create obstacle courses using movable large Loose Parts and challenge each other to tackle the courses.

Many of us have memories of playing outdoors, building forts, finding hiding places, and imagining fantasy worlds. We manipulated our environment and developed complex stories that guided our play. The spaces were messy and perhaps offered a sense of risk that challenged us. When adults experience the flexibility and messiness of pop-up playscapes, they discover innovative ways to think about the world and how it works based on their own self-led, intrinsically motivated interests. This understanding can lead them to value play in young children more and to better support it.

Spend the morning at an adventure playground, or explore a nature space such as a forest, ravine, or botanical garden. Give yourselves permission to play without restrictions and fear. Take risks, challenge yourselves to be in the moment, and get absorbed by the flow.

After the morning play, gather as a group to reflect on the experience.

● How did it feel to be free to explore and play without constraints?

● What did you learn about yourself (such as your expectations, fears, willingness to take risks, and understanding of the value of play)?

● How did the morning change your understanding of the power of play?

Record the answers as a reminder of the importance of embracing play.

Gravel Pits, Mud Puddles, and Sand Spaces

Whenever I ask educators to share a memory of their play growing up, there is always someone who relishes the beloved childhood pastime of splashing, squishing, and running in the mud. There were no rules or guidelines, and the free exploration guided the play. Mud play continues to fascinate adults, who have many ways to engage in the messy and sensorial experience. Spas offer mud baths to heal and relax. International Mud Day has become a yearly experience in many countries throughout the world, featuring mud obstacle courses, races, and mud-themed events. The next time you have a chance to get muddy, I highly encourage you to do so, and I guarantee you will feel great afterward!

● JUST PLAY! CHALLENGE ●

Organize a mud play day for educators. Here are some activities you can try:

MAKING MUD ART

Believe it or not, mud is a wonderful art medium for creating sculptures and paintings. Mud art is mistake-free, giving freedom to our creativity.

● Paint with mud. Provide different types of soil, such as clay soil (lumpy and sticky), sandy soil (dry and gritty), silty soil (wet and sticky), and peaty soil (dark and spongy). I am particularly fond of terra-cotta red soil. It reminds me of the clay ceramics in Tlaquepaque, Jalisco, in Mexico. Each type of mud yields different shades of "mud paint." Place a large painter's tarp or canvas on the floor or hang it on a wall. You can also use an easel with thick paper. Educators then use brushes or their hands to paint.

● Mold and model mud sculptures. Provide baking molds, rings, forms, and pans. Use clay tools to carve, texturize, shape, and cast the mud. Add details to the sculptures with twigs, pebbles, and leaves.

BUILDING WITH MUD

Mud is a common construction element around the world. Mud structures are remarkably durable. Mud also keeps homes and buildings cool.

● Use mud as mortar to build simple and complex structures. Stones, tree branches, and real bricks can be fixed together with mud.

● Construct roadways using rocks, tree branches, and mud. Add tubes and PVC pipes to build waterways and pipelines.

BENEFICIAL MESS

When we look at the benefits of mud play, we realize that the joy makes the mess worthwhile. Embrace the mess—playing with dirt and mud is "mess"essary!

● Try mixing mud with water, grass, and leaves. Making potions in a mud kitchen can elicit memories of childhood summer days.

● Make mud people. They are just like snow people, but the play continues in the summer.

● Have mudball wars. This is just like a snowball fight, but the balls are made with mud.

Sandcastles

I have fond memories of building sandcastles as a child. I remember watching the water approaching my castle and quickly building a ditch to protect the structure. I also remember feeling that when the castle washed away, it was the water telling me that I had to build a new castle.

For me, building sandcastles is a metaphor for our efforts as educators. What a great lesson in growing patience and understanding that time moves fast. We work hard each day, and we invest our time and creativity in designing projects for the children. Some of our efforts are recognized, and others are forgotten. At times we try to safeguard our efforts by building ditches around them. Even when everything is washed away, we are ready to start again the next day. Our focus is on the process because we know the castles will not exist for long. What remains is our commitment and engagement and the relationships we have built, and we are reminded that what matters most is the time we spend together. No wonder sandcastle building is an engaging adult activity. Just go to any beach and you will see adults and children alike creating magnificent castles and entire cities made of sand.

● JUST PLAY! CHALLENGE ●

Organize a sandcastle day. Educators can build sandcastles in a large sandbox in groups or make personal sandcastles in small sandboxes. Using different types of sand can add interest and new challenges as the textures change. One of my favorite types is Jurassic sand; I prefer it because it is dust-free, holds shapes well, and comes in many colors and textures.

Swings, Rocking Chairs, Benches, and Gathering Spaces

Areas to gather with playful seating, such as bench swings, logs, hammocks, and large pillows, can give adults and children a needed respite between play sequences. Swings and hammocks aid relaxation with the feeling of being suspended in air, the gentle back and forth motion, and even the spinning movements.

Adults and children need places to rest and contemplate their day. After a day of play, there is nothing better than gathering in a circle and telling stories. Discuss what you learned, what you experienced, and how the learning will inform your practices.

Adult outdoor play can be extended to community spaces. Establishing relationships with nature conservatories, farms, museums, and parks to coordinate play days, or designing more permanent play spaces for both adults and children can increase adult play opportunities.

Reflections

Walk around the outdoor space . . .

◉ How is the adult represented in the space?

◉ What will you do to make the space more playful for both adults and children?

◉ How will you use the outdoor space to offer adult playtime?

CHAPTER 10

Just Play! with Families

In play we explore, experiment, examine, express our
very selves, we strengthen our bodies, our minds, our
understanding of our changing selves, our changing
relationships, our deepening love. Playing, we change,
adapt to change, create change.

—Bernard De Koven

For some reason, we educators often think that having conferences with
families to discuss their children's progress, sending an email, or writing a
newsletter is the best way to communicate and build relationships. When
I ask educators, "How do you get to know your families?" they often say
they send out a survey assessing families' needs and interests. There may
also be attempts to connect, such as open houses, multicultural potlucks,
and recognition assemblies, when parents come and see their children's

work, briefly say hello to other families, and talk to the educator for a few minutes. Most of these events are organized and implemented by the school without specific collaboration with families beforehand. When my children were in elementary school, I remember sitting at the school desk and listening to the educator tell us what to expect from our children. I honestly had to control myself not to roll my eyes. It felt impersonal and diminishing. I did not hear acceptance and recognition of who we were as a family. I wanted her to see us and ask about *our* dreams and expectations, to take the time to get to know *us* rather than just selling us her program. I wanted to ask questions and get to know other families. I left wondering how much the teacher really knew my child. I wished we had instead explored something the children did throughout the day.

Many programs conduct effective family engagement activities and increase family interactions. However, how many programs create a sense of community for families and help them become friends? This requires a careful examination of the physical, social, emotional, and cognitive spaces. We also must review our policies to make early childhood ecosystems (both private and public) more inclusive and welcoming to families. The purpose is to integrate play as the everyday ethos of family life. Play experiences may also create more open communication between schools and families, strengthening their interactions to allow more strategic plans for ongoing collaboration. More consistent interaction between families creates a supportive community.

As I present on play around the country, I hear teachers say, "The families want me to teach children to read and write," or ask, "How do I convince families that the most important thing for children is to play?" It is time to reconsider how we engage families to see their children's work and have them become advocates of play. Perhaps the key is to allow families to venture into play with their children.

I know that families are busy, and so was I when my children were little. However, I appreciated the few moments in the morning when I dropped them off at nursery school. I enjoyed having a cup of coffee and exchanging conversations with other families and the educators. It energized me and helped me start the day with a more playful attitude. I planned to wake up early and get to the nursery school with enough time to relax and help my daughters transition into the rhythm of the day. It was not easy and required organization, but in the end it was helpful for our family. I hope that more programs relax their schedules and invite families just to play and become part of the ecosystem's community.

Overcoming Barriers to Families' Play

One of the basic tenets of family engagement is to build a sense of well-being. Life unfolds in a dynamic flux of movements and encounters between bodies, imaginations, histories, values, and materials. Families today are experiencing many stressors that affect their well-being—from financial constraints to overly scheduled lives, leaving limited time for play. When we embrace play as a process, we create a zone of well-being where there is greater satisfaction, more flexibility, and a higher level of acceptance of the changes experienced (Lester 2020). When families experience the benefits of play and realize how it helps them create a balance that decreases their stress, many will be more embracing of the value and freedom they get from a playful attitude.

When we create opportunities for families to play, we achieve effective family engagement while demonstrating to families that play is the way children learn. The more families play, the better they understand and value children's play. The more we support adults' need to create and express their thinking, the more importance they will place on listening to and supporting their children's interests. When families observe the children playing while they sit and relax in the ecosystem, they learn to extend play opportunities at home and recognize that play appears casually in the most mundane circumstances.

Using a human-centric approach as the root that centers the way we design both outdoor and indoor environments will help us design ecosystems that support play, equity, and inclusion. Start by knowing the families. What are their strengths? What do they enjoy doing as a family? What skills can they contribute to the ecosystem? Getting to know families with an open mind and an open heart can make a difference in how we support them. Creating play opportunities for families invites us to learn more about diverse cultural perspectives about play. Getting to know families also includes learning about their play archetypes. By knowing how they prefer to play, you can intentionally incorporate play experiences that engage them.

The next step is to let families know that their voices are heard and that they are central to the community. Ultimately, an active community develops where all stakeholders know that learning happens through play. This commitment can help bridge the school and home environment because everyone shares a mindset. Children will experience enhanced learning and well-being due to the concerted efforts to create more play opportunities.

To increase opportunities for family play in schools, we must redesign our current engagement approaches. Building a playful culture will lead to better communication and higher degrees of engagement. Play needs to exist in a continuum through different settings, from home to school to community. This requires schools to plan for family play. In this continuum of experiences, educators and families constantly examine their beliefs about play and playful learning. The continuum between home and school begins by building relationships that are authentic and where families become central to the decisions made in school. Play is valued and seen as the right of everyone, from young children to adults. Educators recognize the efforts happening at home, and families learn to trust educators as they work toward a common goal. All parties involved must share in co-constructing activities that foster creativity through playtime. Think of family engagements as rooted in an immersive process, which involves appropriately challenging activities through which they lose their sense of time. For example, hold family nights where adults share how they played when they were children and talk about what was meaningful to them in the experience. Educators can use this conversation to make connections to how children benefit from play and how learning happens.

Teaching the Importance of Observation

I want to take a moment to acknowledge that families see academics as the pathway to a solid future for their children. Families want their children to succeed, and they may equate that success with their children learning to read, write, and excel academically. They may value play less and thus frown upon play or not understand that children have to play to learn. To build empathy and help families accept that play is the way children learn, we need to make the learning that happens through play visible to them.

One of the most life-changing classes I took in the early years of my career as an educator was a child observation class. Parents (mostly mothers) gathered to learn together as our children played. A knowledgeable parent educator guided our observations and connected children's play to child development. I learned to give children the freedom to play and follow their interests. I learned that children are competent and will climb up a structure when ready. I learned that play has profound meaning. I learned to appreciate children's creative capacities and know when to step in or step out to allow them to direct the play.

If we want families to advocate for play, we must make it visible. I begin by introducing the process of observation when families start in the early childhood program. They learn that observation aims to see children for who they are and not to identify deficits. Writing simple anecdotes helps them create a beautiful and powerful history of their children's intent, imagination, capacities, and thinking. The most beautiful thing for me is observing how children work hard at making sense of the world they inhabit.

Designing Playful Spaces for Families and Children

Imagine that every day when families drop their children off at the early childhood ecosystem, they have a chance to enjoy a cup of coffee or tea and a light snack. Even if they are running late, they can grab something to take with them. When time permits, they can sit with their children and work on a puzzle or draw together, dig a hole in the sandbox, or facilitate a child-initiated game of ball. Families can say hello to other families and share a moment. After a few minutes, they leave for work or other responsibilities, ready to take on the day. They are energized and relaxed, so their creative spirit emerges.

From the moment families enter the early childhood ecosystem, indoors and out, they are invited to play. The front yard beckons families to gather and play with their children. There is a large water table and bubbles and bench swings to rock children as their families say goodbye. A library space holds comfortable sofas where children and families can read books together. Tables have puzzles for families to solve together. Art easels set up at different heights enable both adults and children to easily explore paint media. A clay station invites families and children to discover new textures with the clay and Loose Parts. A pop-up play space calls families to gather as they bring large boxes, pipes, and other large Loose Parts for children to play with. Picnic tables covered with butcher paper invite families and their children to draw together. The picnic table also allows children who did not have time to eat breakfast to have a snack before the day continues. Both the indoor and outdoor spaces engage families in play while also facilitating a healthy transition for children entering the early childhood ecosystem. A drop-off and pickup schedule that offers some flexibility can help the process. When families can drop off at different times, they may find more time to engage in play before they leave for work.

The weather varies greatly in many places, so planning for family play outdoors may present a challenge. Consider how families could gather as they drop off and pick up their children if your climate does not allow you to remain outside year-round. For instance, a school I visited in Princeton, New Jersey, had a large indoor courtyard where events took place and families gathered. The welcoming space was a perfect place for children to transition as they said goodbye to their families.

Playful Moments with Families and Children

One of the most memorable experiences I had when my children were little was a night of adult play at their nursery school. The grown-ups played with blocks, explored a variety of art materials, worked on puzzles, and experienced the qualities of clay. We also spent time outdoors swinging on the swings, building castles in the sand area, getting dirty in the mud, and going up the slide. I remember the laughter and joy that permeated that evening. After we played for about an hour, which seemed too short, we sat to share a meal and reflect on our play experiences. We asked questions and explored different answers about how play supports learning. Of course, most of the families who attended the nursery school already valued and advocated for children's right to play, but hearing one another's perspectives deepened our understanding. At the end of the evening, we started to clean up, and Tim Craig, the director of the program, asked us to leave the evidence of our play with notes to our children telling them that we learned to play at Children's Circle Nursery School. I still remember my daughter's spirited reaction as she jumped up and down and clapped when she found our notes the next day. Her eyes were wide open in disbelief that we actually had played in her school.

Parents and adult family members need time to relax and play without their children for the adults to build relationships. This can be accomplished by organizing parent play nights while providing separate supervision for the children. Another option is to have families take turns watching the children while other adults play. I have seen these relationships grow in programs that strive to build community. It may seem difficult at first, but when families know they will get to meet other people in the community, they are more ready to participate in the play evening.

Play nights became a monthly occurrence in one of the communities I worked with. The families put together potlucks, which was particularly helpful for families who came straight from work. They had dinner with their children and then relaxed as they played games with other families. The same families also got together to organize events to support their local schools.

An adult play night can be as simple as playing charades or trivia and sharing a meal together. The purpose again is to appreciate the power of playfulness and laughter. Here are some other ideas:

- Have a dance night out. Invite a local dance instructor to teach families line dancing or folk dancing. I prefer group dancing because it creates community and encourages single people or those who are more introverted to join comfortably.

- Invite a play coach to guide play engagement activities. Families can ask questions and explore play invitations they can use with their children at home.

- Show a short film on the power of play and discuss with families how they can create play opportunities at home. Changing the tone of family meetings can make a big difference in building community and encouraging families to advocate for play.

- Have an adult art night. You can hire a local artist to give a short lecture on art and then invite families to explore art media.

- Re-create childhood memories. Ask families to share their childhood play memories ahead of time. When they come to adult play night, provide Loose Parts and other materials they can use to re-create their memories. Follow with a reflection to help families connect to the feelings and learning that took place when they played.

- An improv or imaginative playtime can be engaging and fun. Invite an improv troupe or find ideas in improvisational books. Provide fabric and props to enhance the play.

- Reflective questions to share with families include the following:

  - What did you learn as you watched the film on play? How is learning taking place?

  - How did it feel to share your play memory, and how will the play memory guide you to bring more play for children?

  - What do you notice as your children come home after playing all day?

Invite families to take turns organizing casual "mess about" days. Often families spend their weekend time running errands and cleaning their homes to get ready for the next week. A casual messing-about day can allow them to relax and enjoy a respite from mundane daily activities. The messing-about day does not need to be complicated or need extra time to set up. The schedule is flexible, and families can attend the entire time or just come for a short time. The only essential element of the day is playing together and laughing together. See the following box for some ideas for messing-about days.

JUST PLAY! CHALLENGE

BUBBLES

There is something magical about bubbles. They create light rainbows, and chasing them as they float in the air is engaging. Bubbles can be popped, caught, formed, and manipulated to create different shapes. Bubbles also engage people in hypothesizing and scientific thinking.

- Paint with bubbles. Mix liquid watercolors into the bubble solution. Set up a large cotton sheet or piece of butcher paper and let families blow bubbles at it to create a mural.

- Make large bubbles and long bubbles by testing different wands and strings.

- Bring in a children's pool and fill it with bubble solution. Use a hula hoop to make giant bubbles that can envelop the children.

One of the most amazing things I have ever experienced was Bev Bos using a jacuzzi tub adaptor to create a giant wall of bubbles for children to run through. Just make sure you have a lot of towels to wipe their faces.

LARGE STRUCTURES

Invite families to build large structures together using cups, paper, boxes, and cardboard tubes, or challenge one another to see who can make the tallest buildings. Leave messages with provocations written throughout the yard to spark creative structures.

- Build a circular structure.

- Use cardboard ramps to construct a highway that goes over, under, and around.

- Build a catapult to propel Ping-Pong balls into a box.

- Use a variety of small balls to test ramps and learn about speed, gravity, trajectory, weight, and height.

PAINT EXPLORATIONS

Provide a variety of simple provocations to explore the properties of paint.

- Place a painter's canvas on the floor or on a wall. Children can use different sizes of brushes and diluted washable tempera paint to splatter the canvas.

- Provide several (new) plungers, shallow trays or paper plates, and tempera paint for families to paint large sheets of butcher paper.

- Create a pendulum using an old tripod or easel and empty glue bottles. Cut off the base of the bottle and make two holes to thread the string that will hold the bottle as a pendulum. Lay butcher paper under the tripod. Place tempera or liquid watercolor in the bottles. Have children remove or open the glue bottle tip lid and move the pendulum to create their paintings.

ADDITIONAL THEME DAYS

Here are some more ideas that may interest the families you work with:

- Ephemeral or transient art day. Loose Parts and empty frames invite us to explore symmetry, balance, color theory, and other properties of art. Take photos of the work to send home with families.

- Storytelling/symbolic play day. Engage a storyteller to share their talent with families. Storytellers do not need to be professionals. They can be community members. Provide scarves and other symbolic play props for families to create their own stories. Using fabric instead of clothing and costumes can increase symbolic representation and further support cultural values. Add headbands, hair scrunchies, and shoelaces to help secure the material in place.

- Working with wood day. Provide pieces of wood and tools to engage families in designing and creating their ideas three-dimensionally. The families can show their children how to use the tools safely. (This can be previously discussed and facilitated by the educators to ensure that families know how to use the tools.) Provide protective equipment as well.

- Family tracings. Adults and children trace one another's bodies on large sheets of butcher paper. After the tracing is finished, both can fill in the details as they work together to create a portrait. Display the tracings together. Remember that the learning is in the process and not the final product.

These are just a few ideas for "mess about" days. I am sure that your own playfulness will help you create many more. Invite the families to come up with their own ideas and help you organize them. What better way to have ongoing family engagement!

Just Play! at Home

Often schools prepare bags with a selection of books for families to take home and read to children. There is also a trend to send homework assignments, even in preschool. But we know that children learn through play. After all, they didn't need flash cards to learn to speak or walk. Instead, they learned through exploring and experimenting. We must also support families in continuing to create a culture of playfulness at home.

There are multiple opportunities to integrate play opportunities into everyday home life. It begins with the understanding that children play to learn. For instance, when an infant drops an item, they are exploring gravity. Children learn about their bodies and their physical abilities through rough-and-tumble play. They learn about the principles of design and architecture as they build a tower using plastic containers from the kitchen. They discover the functioning of natural ecosystems as they build small world play habitats using items found at home.

Families today are maneuvering new technologies, new values, and new ways of living. Play is also changing rapidly, and children are incorporating new technologies into their play. As adults, we must reimagine play as a dynamic, overlapping process in which a digital experience and imaginary play interact together to create a fluid moment.

Concern about how technology is displacing physical play is ongoing. Families have a big role in shaping their children's play experiences. They can establish a balance between the time children play with digital media and the time they spend playing outdoors or engaged in imaginary play.

Understanding the nuances of technology can help families make informed decisions on how to select it and when to make space for their children to engage with it. I have always been a huge proponent of play. My children spent a lot of hours engaged in exploring, discovering, and experimenting with different forms of play. Technology was limited, and it entered their lives only when they visited other children. My oldest daughter saved money to purchase a Nintendo (with permission). Before we set it up, we researched some games that we could play as a family, and we invested in them. As a family, we played games and had fun together. The reality is that they were less interested in technology than playing with other children in the neighborhood. A rich and diverse mix of physical, creative, emotional, social, digital, and cognitive play in these early years is vital and ensures that children make the most of these rapidly occurring but often fleeting opportunities for growth.

Play brings families together and strengthens their bonds. When families play together, they help one another make sense of the world and build a common understanding that leads to communication and resilience.

● JUST PLAY! CHALLENGE ●

The following are some ideas for families to bring home.

TREASURE HUNTS

Go on an indoor treasure hunt. Look through drawers, closets, kitchen cupboards, and other spaces where you store items and select items that children can play and tinker with. Ask yourself what opportunities the items offer children to construct, engage in dramatic play, design, prototype, or create art. Organize the items for easy access and observe how children play. Incorporate other items as their interest increases and shifts.

Go on an outdoor treasure hunt. Bring a couple of bags on your next walk. Invite children to collect unexpected discoveries, such as rocks, pods, and leaves. (Ensure that you are respecting local rules and private property when you collect nature materials.) When you come home, give children containers to sort and classify their findings. Step back and observe their play.

WAYS TO LET PLAY FLOW

- Offer children engaging tools and materials that support their interests.

- Create spaces where children can spend time designing, exploring, and testing their ideas.

- Slow down and take the time to play and explore.

- Remember that boredom is the beginning of creativity; step back to give children the opportunity to discover their interests.

- Resist the temptation to hover over children, as they need space and time to concentrate and fully engage in exploration. Offer help only when asked.

- Have flexibility in the daily schedule because children need time to play and explore. They also need time to rest.

- Solitude is one of the ways children enter into the realm of creativity. We all need time to reflect.

One of the most treasured activities in our house was exploring the Imagination Trunk. My daughters and their friends spent many hours playing with the scarves, beads, hats, bracelets, and a wide variety of Loose Parts. They used the contents to create complex dramatic play sequences, sometimes putting on theater shows and using metal washers as entry tickets. Other times they would drag the trunk to the backyard to create fairy worlds and fairylands, making fairies from wooden clothespins and pieces of fabric. The scarves became lakes and rivers surrounding the fairylands. My daughters went on walks around the neighborhood to gather pine cones, acorns, and liquid amber balls. These items became houses for the fairies. The trunk was a staple in our household, and the children played with its contents for years. Our extended families and friends contributed to the trunk on a regular basis, donating tin cans, plastic lids, bottle caps, buttons, and many other intriguing and creative Loose Parts. The children's interest was piqued with every addition. I am proud to say that both my daughters are now grown and work in creative industries. They are successful adults and thoughtful people. I attribute many of their skills to their open-ended play.

Reflections

- What play opportunities will you offer families?

- How will you communicate the value of play to families?

- What strategies will you use to rekindle playfulness in families?

- How will you change your approach to family meetings to make them more playful?

CONCLUSION

Where I See Hope

Play is a WISH—Where I See Hope—that we all need to pursue. Play is as crucial for adults as it is for children. It is a fundamental part of being human. It's how we learn, explore, and have fun. It's an essential part of our creativity, helping us to come up with new ideas and find new ways of doing things. Play is an essential part of the creative process. It is a dance between limits and freedom, a chance to explore new ideas and possibilities. When we are playful, we are more open to listening and observing. We give children more opportunities to test ideas and explore freely without constraints imposed by standards. Playfulness is a form of liberation that propels learning and development. When we adults are playful, we create the conditions for children to play. A playful attitude brings more joy into early childhood ecosystems. Play allows us to be more creative, and it is essential for our mental and emotional health. Playfulness brings joy into our lives. When we're playful, we welcome new experiences and we're more likely to laugh. Laughter is one of the best ways to relieve stress, boost our mood, and connect with others. If you're looking for ways to be more creative and bring more joy into your life, make time to play. Play with your children, visit a playground, join a sports team, or just have fun with your friends and family.

The early childhood profession has play and playfulness at its core. It is crucial that we continue to play as adults so that we become strong advocates for play. As a profession we need to reclaim children's right to play, and that requires that educators, policy makers, and other adults involved in child welfare recognize, support, and advocate for play. In other words, supporting play is our professional responsibility and our ethical obligation.

So let's reclaim our playfulness! It just might change the world. My wish for you is that as you read this book you reconnect with your childhood genius. I invite you to design ecosystems that are centered in play and that have a strong commitment to reclaim creativity, playfulness, and joy! Just play!

References

Bateson, Patrick, and Paul Martin. 2015. *Play, Playfulness, Creativity, and Innovation*. Cambridge: Cambridge University Press.

Beloglovsky, Miriam, and Michelle Grant-Groves. 2020. *Design in Mind: A Framework for Sparking Ideas, Collaborations, and Innovation in Early Education*. St. Paul, MN: Redleaf Press.

Brown, Stuart, and Christopher Vaughan. 2009. *Play: How It Shapes the Brain, Opens the Imagination, and Invigorates the Soul*. New York: Penguin. Kindle.

Brown, Tim. 2008. "Tales of Creativity and Play." Filmed at the Serious Play conference. TED Best of the Web, 27:38. www.ted.com/talks/tim_brown_tales _of_creativity_and_play.

Bruner, Jerome. 1986. "Play, Thought and Language." *Prospects* 16, no. 1 (March): 77–83. https://doi.org/10.1007/bf02197974.

Bruner, Jerome S., Kathy Sylva, and Alison Jolly, eds. 1985. *Play: Its Role in Development and Evolution*. New York: Penguin.

Burghardt, Gordon M. 2006. *The Genesis of Animal Play: Testing the Limits*. Cambridge, MA: MIT Press. https://direct.mit.edu/books/oa-monograph /4951/The-Genesis-of-Animal-PlayTesting-the-Limits.

Csikszentmihalyi, Mihaly. 1997. *Finding Flow: The Psychology of Engagement with Everyday Life*. New York: Basic Books.

Dawson, V. L., Thomas D'Andrea, Rosalinda Affinito, and Erik L. Westby. 1999. "Predicting Creative Behavior: A Reexamination of the Divergence between Traditional and Teacher-Defined Concepts of Creativity." *Creativity Research Journal* 12 (1): 57–66. https://doi.org/10.1207/s15326934crj1201_7.

DeBenedet, Anthony T. 2018. *Playful Intelligence: The Power of Living Lightly in a Serious World*. Solana Beach, CA: Santa Monica Press.

De Koven, Bernard. 2014. *A Playful Path*. ETC Press.

de Saint-Exupéry, Antoine. 2019. *The Little Prince*. Classica Libris. Kindle.

Durkin, Kelly, Mark W. Lipsey, Dale C. Farran, and Sarah E. Wiesen. 2022. "Effects of a Statewide Pre-Kindergarten Program on Children's Achievement and Behavior through Sixth Grade." *Developmental Psychology* 58 (3): 470–84. https://doi.org/10.1037/dev0001301.

Erickson Institute. 2016. "Technology and Young Children in the Digital Age." www.erikson.edu/wp-content/uploads/2018/07/Erikson-Institute-Technology -and-Young-Children-Survey.pdf.

Gilliam, Walter S., Angela N. Maupin, Chin R. Reyes, Maria Accavitti, and Frederick Shic. 2016. "Do Early Educators' Implicit Biases regarding Sex and Race Relate to Behavior Expectations and Recommendations of Preschool Expulsions and Suspensions?" Yale University, Child Study Center. https:// medicine.yale.edu/childstudy/zigler/publications/Preschool%20Implicit% 20Bias%20Policy%20Brief_final_9_26_276766_5379_v1.pdf.

Hendricks, Barbara E. 2011. *Designing for Play (Design and the Built Environment).* 2nd ed. New York: Routledge. Kindle.

Hoicka, Elena, Jessica Joelle Alexander, Zhen Wu, and Bo Stjerne Thomsen. 2018. "Lego Play Well Report." The Lego Foundation. https://cms.learningthrough play.com/media/3oyhmaud/lego-play-well-report-2018.pdf.

Huizinga, Johan. 1950. *Homo Ludens: A Study of Play-Element in Culture.* Reprint ed. Boston: Beacon Press.

Lester, Stuart. 2020. *Everyday Playfulness: A New Approach to Children's Play and Adult Responses to It.* Philadelphia: Jessica Kingsley.

Magnuson, Cale D., and Lynn A. Barnett. 2013. "The Playful Advantage: How Playfulness Enhances Coping with Stress." *Leisure Sciences*, 35 (2): 129–44.

Montagu, Ashley. 1989. *Growing Young.* 2nd ed. Granby, MA: Bergin & Garvey. Kindle.

Pellis, Sergio, Vivien Pellis, and Heather Broccard-Bell. 2011. "The Function of Play in the Development of the Social Brain." *American Journal of Play.* 278–96.

Proyer, René T. 2017. "A New Structural Model for the Study of Adult Playfulness: Assessment and Exploration of an Understudied Individual Differences Variable." *Personality and Individual Differences* 108 (April 1): 113–22. https:// doi.org/10.1016/j.paid.2016.12.011.

Reddan, Marianne C., Tor D. Wager, and Daniela Schiller. 2018. "Attenuating Neural Threat Expression with Imagination." *Neuron* 100 (4): 994–1005. https:// doi.org/10.1016/j.neuron.2018.10.047.

Ryan, Richard M., and Edward L. Deci. 2000. "Self-Determination Theory and the Facilitation of Intrinsic Motivation, Social Development, and Well-Being." *American Psychologist* 55, no. 1 (January): 68–78. https://doi.org/10.1037 /0003-066x.55.1.68.

Sawyer, R. Keith. 1997. *Pretend Play as Improvisation: Conversation in the Preschool Classroom.* Mahwah, NJ: Lawrence Erlbaum. Kindle.

Westgate, Erin C., Timothy D. Wilson, Nicholas R. Buttrick, Rémy A. Furrer, and Daniel T. Gilbert. 2021. "What Makes Thinking for Pleasure Pleasurable?" *Emotion* 21 (5): 981–89. https://doi.org/10.1037/emo0000941.

Index

CPSIA information can be obtained
at www.ICGtesting.com
Printed in the USA
JSHW060232260523
42225JS00001B/1